The Pocket Stylist

Behind-the-Scenes Expertise from a Fashion Pro
on Creating Your Own Unique Look

Kendall Farr

Illustrations by
Anja Kroencke

GOTHAM BOOKS

For my husband George

**My left brain, and a man who is indifferent
to hemlines, unless they are very short**

Gotham Books
Published by Penguin Group (USA) Inc.
375 Hudson Street, New York, New York 10014, U.S.A.
Penguin Books Ltd, Registered Offices: 80 Strand, London WC2R 0RL, England
Penguin Books Australia Ltd, 250 Camberwell Road, Camberwell, Victoria 3124, Australia
Penguin Books Canada Ltd, 10 Alcorn Avenue, Toronto, Ontario, Canada M4V 3B2
Penguin Books (NZ) Ltd, Cnr Rosedale and Airborne Roads, Albany, Auckland 1310,
      New Zealand

Published by Gotham Books, a division of Penguin Group (USA) Inc.

First printing, February 2004
10 9 8 7 6 5 4

Gotham Books and the skyscraper logo are trademarks of Penguin Group (USA) Inc.

Library of Congress Cataloging-in-Publication Data

Farr, Kendall, 1959–
    The pocket stylist : behind-the-scenes expertise from a fashion pro on creating your own
unique look / by Kendall Farr.
        p.   cm.
    ISBN 1-592-40041-8 (hardcover : alk. paper)
    1. Clothing and dress. 2. Fashion. 3. Beauty, Personal. 4. Image consultants. I. Title
    TT507.F325 2004
    646'.34—dc22   2003019229

Printed in the United States of America
Set in New Caledonia Family and Helvetica Neue Family
Designed by Susi Oberhelman

This book is printed on acid-free paper. ∞

contents

introduction

Few things are more seductive than *fashion*—the transformative quality of clothes that really fit and flatter us. New clothes offer us the potential to reinvent ourselves a little bit each time we get dressed. Wearing a great outfit provides salvation on a lousy day, armor for the tough meeting, the courage to walk into a cocktail party full of strangers. Our choice of clothing can be one of our most creative forms of self-expression. The colors and shapes we wear telegraph how we see ourselves. Like it or not, in a rabidly visual, image-obsessed world we're assessed in nanoseconds, dozens of times per day, based on what we are wearing.

I have been a fashion stylist for over fifteen years yet I often feel that when reading the top women's fashion magazines, I have come in in the middle of a conversation. If I have this sensation (being familiar with all the references) it's no wonder that so many women are mystified by fashion coverage that seems to be aimed at "It" girls, socialites, and actresses.

Somehow, good advice is not getting through to many women. I see evidence of this every day: women dressed in clothes that don't fit properly or don't suit the shapes of their bodies. A whopping disconnect exists between what women read in fashion magazines or see on celebrity style television and what they really need to know about dressing themselves well.

I've written *The Pocket Stylist* to be your style compass in a confusing fashion terrain. You can and will be a woman who knows how to shop for the best shapes and fit for her individual shape. You can be the savvy girl who knows how to mix well-edited trends with your classic pieces. Real personal style often has little to do with what is considered fashionable in any season (or week). Style is a state in which a woman's own sense of what works for her body, and what does not, overrides the marketing hysteria that ushers in the newest, hottest, must-haves. Style is not only the province of iconic swans like Audrey Hepburn or Jacqueline Onassis, it is learned behavior and a simple and gradual process of training your eye to lock onto your best silhouettes and proportions in any season, any year. For now, however, let's start with three of women's biggest misconceptions about fashion.

Big Fashion Misconception #1

To truly look great in your clothing you must maintain a model's figure. Ludicrous, not to mention really unhealthy. High-fashion models, the anointed superstars of the runways and magazines, are the rarest of body types. Many are built straight up and down like boys, but with boobs and broad shoulders. Their preternatural shapes are one in several million, the genetic equivalent of winning the lottery. Rationally, we all know this, but we live in a culture that barrages us every day with the message that extreme thinness is the body ideal of any stylish woman. Your only fashion ideal should be you at your best, and that means well-dressed for your body as it is now—not ten pounds from now, or six months of Pilates from now, but right *now*.

Big Fashion Misconception #2

Your style quotient is raised whenever you wear the must-haves of any season—wearing the BIG LOOKS assures that you look like you have an insider view of fashion. Just not true. Hunting down the latest runway looks—original or adapted—with no regard for how they'll look on your individual proportions is where style ends and fashion enslavement begins.

The woman without a realistic sense of what fashion can and cannot do for her wastes her money, drives herself crazy trying to get a look, and often still feels like nothing in her closet really works. We've all seen her: The logos are mixed and matched; she's an unrestrained cowgirl; a new romantic; flouncy in folklorica; or a rock chick on the prowl in crotch-high leopard and platforms. She's a walking billboard for the sensibilities of a design house or has embraced, all too literally, what is promoted in fashion magazines, but she hasn't cracked the code of truly individual style.

Consider two characters from HBO's *Sex and the City* as examples. Carrie Bradshaw, whose wardrobe schizophrenia establishes her as the fashion risk taker of the group is, from a costume design perspective, a vividly drawn character and memorable in every scene. From a style perspective, she's fashion's prisoner. In an early episode, one of Carrie's outfits consisted of a Salvation Army cape that swamped her small frame (yes, capes were spotted on the runway at that moment and yes, her thrift variation was meant to bestow a kind of insider credibility on this getup), and was accessorized with white gloves and a silk flower the size of a satellite dish on her lapel; she was teetering, as always, in skyscraping stilettos.

Charlotte, on the other hand, has figured out how to dress as a stylish individual. Her look is current, not slavish: a Prada skirt here, a Chloé top there, suggesting that she has an eye for trends, but wears them selectively. Her clothes fit her perfectly in part because they fit her proportions.

Don't get me wrong: Seasonal trends can be irresistible. They infuse excitement into an often monotonous landscape of basics and clothing that looks the same season after season. But a little bit of a good thing may be enough. I'll show you how to choose what works for you.

Big Fashion Misconception #3

Ready-to-wear actually is ready to wear. In fact, an affordable perfect fit right off the rack is as impossible to find as a Hermès Birkin bag on sale. Great tailoring (and thus clothes that fit you perfectly) is the single most critical factor in raising your style profile. One universal truth about women with great personal style is that their clothes fit—*really* fit. I'll show you how to find a tailor wherever you live, and how to ask for the alterations that will transform the fit of your clothes from passable to perfect.

I love fashion magazines. They are visually exciting and can be great entertainment, but their mission is not to instruct you. Their job is to report what is new and what's next. Their goal is to produce exciting fashion pages—and to service their advertisers. Selling ads keeps them in business. When a designer spends a lot of money on advertising, implicit in the bargain are numerous editorial mentions. Entire stories may promote his or her newest designs, meaning that much of the information and advice you get will always be weighted in the direction of the designers with the deepest pockets (regardless of the appeal of their collections). Ever notice that those token runway-to-reality-clothes-for-your-figure charts include mostly advertisers' clothing? That's business, but it can be a problem if it misleads and confuses us into buying stuff that is flat-out wrong for our individual shapes and proportions.

Let's not shoot the messengers, however. Designers need to sell clothes. They need to create runway buzz every six months to capture the attention of an excruciatingly jaded fashion press, store buyers, and assorted tastemakers who they hope will photograph, buy, and wear their newsmaking riffs on the new season.

This is no mystery to me. I've styled many stories for fashion magazines and been a part of this very cycle, so I realize just how confusing fashion can be. As often as not, the gulf between what makes exciting images and what you'll want to wear—and invest your money in—can be wide indeed. Add to that the celebrity factor: The media (entertainment television in particular) that covers the fashion beat has transformed getting dressed (as it relates to Oscar nominees and pop stars) into high drama. Why? Because fashion draws in women and we read, we watch, we listen, and we buy things—to the tune of billions of dollars annually.

This showbiz view of fashion as consisting of red-carpet clothes, tour wardrobes, and sitcom costumes, has established the actress as arbiter of style. Most actresses I've worked with have enough pressure just performing their jobs. That the media focuses on them as de facto runway models every time they walk a press line or attend a party has produced an over-the-top, near hysterical take on fashion that couldn't be less relevant to real personal style. Style doesn't come with proximity to celebrity; it comes from knowing yourself. That's where I come in.

what is a stylist?

In my career as a fashion stylist I've spent years learning about women's bodies, and the fabrics, styles, and fit that will create gorgeous images in front of the camera. I'm hired for my eye—an ability to distill what I see on the runways, on the street, in films, in magazines, and to translate trends into clothing and accessory options for my clients. I spend time with private clients helping women figure out their personal style and choosing clothes that complement their body types and lifestyles. Whether you're a size 2 or 22, you can use a simple formula for finding the best possible proportion and fit to build a wardrobe that enhances your appearance.

Within my job description, I wear many hats. As a freelance fashion editor, who has produced stories for magazines here and in Europe, I conceive of a story idea (using a trend of the season) and choose the best clothes and accessories to illustrate the idea. I then choose the photographer, the hair-and-makeup team, and the model who will make it all come alive on the page. For print and television advertising, I choose the wardrobe that creates a stylish image of the woman who uses a product. Even when all you see on your screen is a flash of a neckline or a quick glimpse of an outfit, it is the result of racks of clothing options that have been considered by the team—the photographer-director of the ad or commercial, the art director from the ad agency, and the client—to arrive at just the right look. I've dressed actresses for all kinds of magazine shoots (both as models for fashion stories and for glammed-up portraits to promote their latest films) and as private clients for the Academy Awards, the Golden Globes, and the Cannes Film Festival. I've styled album covers for pop singers and opera singers alike, and on-camera wardrobe for talk show hosts, newscasters, and sports figures. Altogether, they represent a wide array of bodies from petite women like Julie Bowen and Courtney Thorne-Smith; to curvy women like Halle Berry, Cindy Crawford, and Angelina Jolie; to tall women like Diane Sawyer, Sigourney Weaver, Andie McDowell, Connie Nielsen, and Mandy Moore; to full-figured women like models Emme, Kate Dillon, and *The View* host Star Jones.

WORKING WITH WOMEN over the years, I've been asked the same question again and again: Why can't I shop for myself as well as a stylist shops for me? You can. I have written *The Pocket Stylist* to help any woman of any shape and size to shop for and wear the clothes that will fit and flatter her best. Think of this guide as *your own personal stylist*, on hand for a consultation whenever you shop. *The Pocket Stylist* has been designed to guide you through an understanding of fashion's fundamentals: the elements of proportion, fabric, and color that are the tools that designers use to make clothing that has line, shape, drape. You will come to know how these elements relate to your best silhouettes in any season, in any year.

I'll show you how to edit your closet and replace the discards with pieces that will raise your style quotient. We'll go on a virtual shopping trip and make choices together. I outline specifically how I shop for my private clients—and myself—and the indispensables no well-conceived wardrobe can be without. We will talk about the trends that resurface with regularity and that are worth investing in.

I'll discuss finding a good tailor and show you how to talk to him or her. Custom-made pieces are the stylist's secret weapon; you'll see how simple, satisfying, and unintimidating this process can be, particularly for women who find a good fit hard to find.

I will explore the critical connection between wardrobe, hair, and makeup and how all these things must work together for a woman's best style to emerge. Advice from hairstylist, author, and *Allure* columnist Kevin Mancuso makes it simple to get a good haircut. Bobbi Brown, makeup expert and CEO of Bobbi Brown Professional Cosmetics, explains how to find your perfect foundation and concealer, and then what to do with them! Sonia Kashuk, makeup artist and author, shares her tips for choosing the right tools and discusses classic combinations for lips and cheeks. Dida Paraschivoiu, the eyebrow and manicure guru behind the scenes of beauty commercials and fashion magazine shoots, explains perfect arches and nail tips.

I weigh in with my favorite foundation pieces for underneath-it-all for all sizes (straight from my kit bag), plus other tricks of the trade. The old saw about buying this season's hottest accessories and wearing them with clothes from past seasons only works when a woman understands context, proportion, and scale, and you'll learn how to bring a look together with accessories in all price ranges, as well as what to look for in investment jewelry new and old.

The Pocket Stylist is a portable guide to help you create a versatile wardrobe, assemble a closet balanced between well-edited trends and stylish practicality, and decide when to break the bank and when to save your money. Read on: you are now my client. Let's open my kit bag, metaphorically speaking, and start developing your "eye," so you can learn to shop for yourself like a pro. ●

1 form and fashion

The first thing I do when choosing any piece of clothing for a photo shoot is to visualize how the cut will fit the body. Will the silhouette flatter the subject's shape and size? Will the fabric drape and smooth over her contours? Will the color(s) flatter her skin tone? Are there any interesting details that set it apart from the ordinary? Only after all this do I consider its place in the current trends landscape. Because, frankly speaking, that is the least important factor in how it will look on the subject's body or yours.

In this chapter, I'll ask you to look at your own clothes this way. Since the last rule left in fashion is that there are no rules, a girl first needs to have the clearest possible understanding of her body in order to pull her wardrobe together. To train your eye for your best options, you need to know the basic principles that designers use to construct the clothing you wear. Our work together begins with a brief glossary of fashion fundamentals.

SILHOUETTE: Outline of an outfit (picture a black cameo against a white background), its shape and cut. Designers first express their ideas for a season with the silhouettes they send down the runway. Most important, think of silhouette as *the outlined shape or contour of your body* and what will flatter it best.

PROPORTION: Individual pieces of an outfit in relation to one another. On the runways, the seasonal combinations of long with short, wide with narrow, tight with loose, that designers devise to keep things new, and which instantly relegate the trendy portions of our wardrobes to obsolete. Examples: a cropped jacket with wide-leg trousers, midthigh-length coat worn with knee-length pencil skirt. Most important, think about proportion in the context of *your body proportions* and how the clothes and accessories you choose can work in scale and balance with your individual size and shape.

FABRIC: Naturally, you know what fabric is, but you might not know that it must complement and support the silhouette. For example, an A-line skirt or gored skirt in cotton twill has pup tent potential, whereas the same shapes in midweight jersey will drape and move with your body. Pay close attention to the surface quality of fabric, since weaves that add texture to a garment can also add some very unflattering bulk; a surface with shine adds more volume than a matte finish. Some examples: flat versus boucle or mohair wools; matte jersey, which drapes and skims versus high-sheen satin jersey, which adds width and outlines every lump and bump. Matte stretch fabrics and lycra are a girl's (of any size) friend and ally. Fabric is critical to supporting the line of tailored clothing and this is where cheap stuff is the most telling. (We'll talk about when to spend on better fabrics and when bargains will work just fine in chapter 4.)

OPTICAL ILLUSION VERSUS DELUSION: All women should worship the **almighty unbroken line.** Meaning, we're always looking for silhouettes and proportions that will create the longest-looking body line. This also means that if a "must-have" piece you've clocked in the fashion pages doesn't help you achieve the vertical line it created on the model, you'll leave it in the dressing room and look for a version of the idea that works for you.

Think about these qualities before you worry about whether or not a piece of clothing falls into one of the big trends of the season. This is important to keep in mind, since the idea of anything this basic (but critical) can all but dissolve when you try to navigate the floors of a department store. Listen, I do this for a living and I sometimes feel like I've been caught in a windstorm of *must-have big looks.* I see racks filled with silly, shrunken proportions, crotch-high skirts, butt-crack-grazing jeans, tricky constructions and details, and versions of the same shapes, colors, and prints from label to label. (This is not fashion telepathy, by the way. Design companies subscribe to trend-forecasting services that provide much of the style prescience needed to predict what we girls may want a year in the future.)

Lots of **best of the season** fashion ideas seem crazy to me in their disregard of what it means for a woman to move comfortably in her clothes. As I've said before, the ways in which designers tweak and change silhouettes and proportions each season is what keeps fashion interesting (and keeps us buying). But a little of a trend can go a long way and it's often best expressed with accessories (we'll get there in chapter 7). Remember, *a trend is only relevant for you if it has a shape that fits and flatters your body.* In fact, there are only two kinds of clothes in the fashion universe: those that fit and flatter your body shape and size, and those that don't. Simple, right? There are many ways for a girl to express an individual sense of style without looking like a fashion casualty. The best place to begin is to make trends work for you, rather than trying to turn yourself inside out to adapt to whatever designers are pushing in any season.

What distinguishes good fit for any body at any size? Clothing that skims the outline of your shape. Nothing clings or pulls, nor is anything so oversized that it hides your body's natural outline. When I look at clothing on a body that's in motion in front of the camera, I watch how the construction, fabric, and fit look in a three-dimensional, circular sense; how the front blends into the sides, around to the back, and to the front again, whether the wearer is walking, sitting, or just standing. Is anything pulling, puckering, gapping, or bagging? The next time you put on your favorite pair of pants and a fitted jacket or button-front shirt, rotate slowly in front of your own mirror (try this in heels, please), stand up straight, and roll your shoulders back to add instant length and posture. Stand, walk in place, sit, and pay attention to the following areas.

- Wherever buttons close
- Across your bust
- Bra lines under your arms and across your back
- Around the armholes
- Across your sleeves and shoulders
- Across your stomach
- Fabric across your hips and belly
- Across your bottom and crotch

If any of these places are visibly tight or loose or if you see deep, obvious creasing or gapping, the line of the outfit in total will be thrown off. *The line and fit of your clothing are critical elements of your personal style.* Regardless of how much you've paid for something or whose name is on the label, bad fit is never going to flatter your body shape. If it's not flattering, what's the point of wearing it? For that matter, what's the point of buying it?

We all have a tendency to define ourselves by the parts of our anatomy that give us the most grief in the fitting room. And why wouldn't we? Everything we've ever read about *dressing for our body types* deconstructs our bodies, one part at a time, into a series of *hot spots.* None of us is our boobs, butts, hips, or thighs; rather, we are uniquely the sum of our parts. Yet just about every woman I know and many I've worked with (yes, many famous women, including models who are paid for their proportions) will immediately talk to me about her perceived hot spots. Trust me, this is not the first step to understanding the shape of your body. Shopping for clothing fixated on one body part rather than considering your silhouette is a recipe for disappointment. This hot-spot body insecurity is just one more way that we women can be self-defeating when it comes to making good fashion judgments. Not anymore.

For now, I'll ask you to suspend all of what you think you know about the shape of your body. I don't know about you, but I've never found it particularly *instructive* to think about my body as a piece of fruit or as a geometry exercise. For now, please forget about every hinky chart or graph you've ever followed, along with every inane so-called figure fixer tip you've learned since high school, and shift this to a completely spatial perspective. I'll ask you to look at yourself straight on (in a bra and panties, please) in a full-length mirror and absorb this: you are your frame—your *silhouette*—first. Your individual *measurements*, which refine your *fit,* come second.

Coco Chanel said it well: "Fashion is architecture: it is a matter of proportions." Like architecture, we are looking at your natural frame. Your size may go up and down in your life but your frame is constant. When I have an initial fitting with a client, I first look at the shape of her torso facing me straight on. So, let's now focus on the shape of your torso. Visualize a dress form: shoulders to hips (not

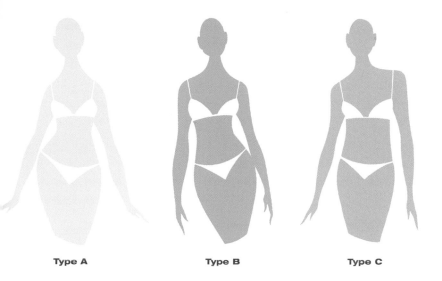

| Type A | Type B | Type C |

by coincidence the very tool that fashion designers use when they create clothing silhouettes). Designers have to conceive the shapes—the silhouettes—before they consider how a woman's individual measurements will factor into the equation. It is your **torso silhouette** that will basically determine the line and the clothing shapes that are best for your body. Although we all hold weight differently and have different sized breasts, in general I've encountered the same three combinations of torso proportions that illustrate our first three **body types: A, B, and C.** Body types D, E, and F have the same basic proportions as A, B, and C but represent plus-sized bodies. Here's how to find your body type.

- Is the width of your shoulders and torso smaller than the width of your hips? **You are a Type A.**

- Are your shoulders and your hips roughly the same width, with a defined waist? **You are a Type B.**

- Is the width of your shoulders the same or wider than the width of your hips with little definition at your waist? **You are a Type C.**

Remember that body types D, E, and F represent women who are fuller variations on A, B, and C. Body type D is a voluptuous, *full-fashion* version of body type A, E of B, and F of C. Your body type as defined by your torso silhouette is the very best initial determination of *your most flattering shapes and body line, at any size*. You can be a size 8 body type B or a size 14W body type E and many of the clothing shapes, focal points, and balance recommendations will be the same for both and the best route to finding your most flattering looks.

As you stand in front of your mirror, take in *a spatial impression of your whole body*, meaning the relationship between all of your body parts. Now we'll also consider the size of your neck, the size of your breasts, the size of your booty, and the length and shape of your legs. With these features in mind let's concentrate on your individual measurements.

Now I'll ask you to do something that you'll probably resist: measure yourself. Stand up straight, roll your shoulders back to open up your chest, and *really look at your body*. Take in the full view, not just your front and back. Consider your circularity, the three-dimensional quality of your body in all its glory. Having this visual picture in your head—an awareness of your body size and shape—is essential to making the right choices for yourself when you shop.

Okay, now take your measurements and fill in the appropriate spaces provided here (in pencil, as these will change over time). *A handy tip straight from Parsons School of Design*: with the exception of your shoulders and your rise, always hold two fingers under your tape measure to build in the right amount of ease.

- **Shoulder to Shoulder:** From the edge of one shoulder to the edge of the other shoulder. 16 1/2
- **Bust:** under your arms, around the fullest part of your chest. 32 1/2
- **Natural waist:** At your navel . 29
- **Low waist:** Approximately one inch down from your natural waist. 30
- **High Hip:** 4 to 5 inches: from your natural waist. 32
- **Low Hip:** 8 to 9 inches: from your natural waist. 36
- **Thigh:** At its widest point. 21
- **Rise:** Measure from natural waist down to crotch, holding the tape a little loose, through the legs up to waistband in back; repeat for low waist. 26
  23 1/2

Stay with me. If we were working together in real life, this is *exactly* how we would begin—with a fitting—and start the process of finding what's best for your individual shape and size. And I'd ask to measure you after you'd had a healthy lunch so that I'd get the most accurate read of your body (not to mention that all of us, at any size, retain more fluid by afternoon). Yes, girls, *more joys of womanhood.* Taking and understanding these measurements will help you think about your *entire body proportionately* and will help you find better fit. I promise.

Unless you commit to the few minutes this takes, the very specific shopping list that I've created for your body type in the next chapter simply won't have as much value for you. I promise again: looking at your measurements on the page as a gauge of your proportions is the best way to find fit. Refer to your measurements when you shop in stores, in catalogues, or on the Internet, and stop worrying about arbitrary size tags.

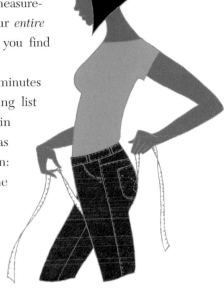

Measuring your rise

the size enigma

If finding your size seems more difficult than ever, or if you wonder why your size can vary from manufacturer to manufacturer, let me assure you that the problem is not you. It's the process of pattern-making for the mass market. Here's how a designer friend explained it to me: Patterns of any size, let's say size 8, for example, are a standardized averaging of every conceivable variance within a range of measurements.

Seventh Avenue's biggest manufacturers base their data on what their market research tells them about "their" woman: her height on average; her weight on average; bust, waist, and hips on average. They hire fit models whose proportions best simulate the number averages. The obvious goal for the manufacturer is to try to fit as many of us within the size as possible. This does not mean fit *well.* In fact, sizing is an inexact science at best, which means that finding great fit off the rack is a crapshoot. It usually translates as your body's resemblance to the fit model's shape. It's best to think of ready-to-wear as *almost ready-to-wear,* since it almost never fits perfectly without at least some minor alterations.

vanity sizing

Another wrinkle in the fit system is vanity sizing; it's the reason your regular size can hang off your frame in some lines and fit you reasonably well in others. As manufacturers struggle to keep up with the expansion of the average American backside they downsize their size tags—great for our heads but confusing and time-consuming for finding the right fit. Always try things on until you find the lines that cut things for your combination of proportions.

buyer beware

Why do clothes look beautifully tailored and great fitting when you see them in fashion stories, in ads, and in catalogues? Because a stylist manipulates what is often a poorly fitting sample to look expensive and perfectly tailored. In general, if something is too small, I open up the back seams and fill them in with a piece of cloth (known as a *gusset*). More often, things are huge and require tailoring with large safety pins or quick stitches. Shoulderlines and necks are pulled in; arms, pant legs, and skirts are narrowed and pinned or basted down the back to create a shape and drape that doesn't exist otherwise. If a lapel or placket won't lie flat, a little toupee tape under the offending area solves the problem nicely. The stylist and the photographer work together to figure out the best possible angle to photograph this pinned, taped creation and *voilà*: the *appearance* of an irresistible piece of clothing.

NOW, ARMED WITH YOUR MEASUREMENTS and tape measure, let's go shopping, say, for a pair of pants. As you reach for something in your size, hold it up and really look at the construction. Does it look like the right size? Not sure? *Measure it.* Try a flat-front pant, for example. Run your tape across the pant front at the low hip and multiply by two. Then measure the rise at the natural or low waist, depending on the style. If you're in the ballpark in both places, head to the fitting room. If not, move up or down a size and don't think about the number on the tag—it's far less relevant than finding you a pair of pants that slides over your body without pulling or hanging off your frame. If you've fit your hips and bottom but the waist is big, pinch the fabric at either side of the waistband (which is just what a tailor will do when he takes them in so that they fit perfectly, but more on this in chapter 5). Now, double-check the rise. It shouldn't feel short in the crotch or hang low. If you slide a pair of pants down to sit lower on your hips than they have been cut to do, check that crotch: if it's hanging too low it's not a pretty sight. Adjusting the rise can be tough for even the most skilled tailor to remedy.

Try this same series of measurements when you look for jeans but also measure the thigh, since this is often an area deceptively slimmer than it appears on the hanger. As we've all experienced, the jeans market defines inconsistency in sizing. The formula for a slim skirt is the same as for pants: lower hip times two.

Your stylist would rather have an MRI than spend any more time than necessary in a fitting room, particularly for no good reason. Measuring works; it will save your time and your sanity. If you've ever grabbed a pair of pants based on the size tag alone, only to squeeze into what felt like a sausage casing, you know what I mean.

How and why did I begin measuring the hell out of everything? In a word: actresses. I dress a lot of them for magazines and advertising. I've often had nothing more to go on until the day of the shoot than the sizes their publicists or managers provided. Yes, in the infancy of my career, I endured a few joyless shoots because I trusted sizes alone. (Naturally, I now insist on a list of current measurements.) Buy a tape measure for your purse and keep it there (along with *The Pocket Stylist,* of course).

This is a process! As we hone your eye for your best proportions, think about your measurements first, in whatever you look at and ultimately decide to try on. Let's move on to chapter 2 for a more specific rundown of your body type and an edited shopping list of your best clothing options. ●

2 what's right for your body type?

If you've read this far, then you understand that clothing is designed for silhouette first and measurements second. I'll mention this again (yes, count on me to flog this point throughout the book): your *silhouette*, the essential frame you are born with, is the beginning of any conversation you have with clothes. Our measurements change—they naturally go up and down in a lifetime and they can be changed considerably with exercise and diet—but your frame remains the one constant in the equation.

Your edited list, from bottoms to tops, is based on what I have found to be the right shapes for your frame. How do I define *right*? Naturally, it's an assessment based on what will streamline your body and give you the *almighty unbroken line* I mentioned earlier. When a woman develops her eye to choose and adapt clothing that best flatters her particular shape—not an idealized shape—she has also tapped into a timeless aesthetic of *balance, proportion, and line*. In your stylist's opinion, this is the foundation of real personal style. Forget the vagaries of fashion, let's concentrate on elevating your reality.

As you flip to your body type and read through your list of shapes and proportions, keep this in mind: this is not just a shopping list for this season—think of this as your list for *any season, any year.* There are only so many ways to skin a cat. Remember, designers don't reinvent silhouettes every season, they reexamine them and tweak them a bit for newness. So, when you know what you're looking for, you will always spot seasonal reinterpretations of *your* shapes as you shop. You'll also find four illustrated looks that combine ideal silhouettes and proportions from casual to cocktails, which can serve as a visual blueprint for the shopping ahead.

for all body types

Shape should be at work in any piece of clothing you choose: what you want to downplay or de-emphasize you'll want to dress simply, without a lot of details that draw in the eye. What you want to highlight and expose are places for detail, color, embellishment, something trendy. I'll elaborate on all of this as we move along.

I recommend that every body type wear her skirts at knee length. Visually you know your own best hem length is the point at which your legs look their longest and slimmest. Whether yours is just above or just below the knee, *at the knee* is a general guideline for a length that will show off your legs at their best. If you've got great legs, by all means raise your hemline a bit when shorts skirts are a part of the trends landscape. A caveat, however: stand with your hands by your side and make sure that your hem reaches the tip of your middle finger. If it doesn't, your skirt is disproportionately short for your height (not to mention a little tarty-looking). I'll outline the best shapes in skirts—at various lengths—for your body type.

As you read on, you'll see that I recommend a low waistline (hits about 1″ to 1½″ below your navel for average sizing and at the navel for full-fashion sizing) for pants and jeans. If you a have a rounded abdomen (and who doesn't at least once a month, a day, an hour?) a waistband that sits high on your waist appears to mold fabric around your belly. A low waistline creates the illusion of a longer torso and, by placing a horizontal line through the fullness, the illusion of a flatter stomach.

You'll also see that I emphasize hemming your pants to wear with heels to lengthen your body line and raise your rear view. Honestly ladies, I am not a sadist. I know there are times when you must be built for speed and comfort and that means wearing flats or sneakers. But a girl must have different hem lengths in her closet; including at least a few pairs of pants with a killer fit that you can throw on with *at least* a kitten heel to look a little longer and leaner.

To my eye, sleeveless and cap-sleeve tops are not your friends at any size unless your arms are toned. For the millions of us that do not have toned arms—or who hold weight in our arms—our best bet is to cover them. Think about it, the eye is immediately drawn to any expanse of skin. The skin you show off should flatter your overall silhouette. Create the illusion of sleeker, longer arms with lengths at three-quarter and with styles like handkerchief, kimono, or cape sleeves that fall midarm to elbow. Use sleeveless as a layering option. I don't want to rain on your comfort parade, but it's my job to make sure you choose what creates your optimum line.

body types D, E, and F

The girls represented by body types D, E, and F are women of size and stature and who have voluptuous, full curves. You may shop 14, 16, or 18 in missy lines or 12W or larger in plus-size lines. I'll preface your edited shapes with a few of the things we'll consider—and avoid—as we shop.

▶ We're looking for individual pieces that enhance focal points: the neck and shoulders, back, cleavage, forearms, legs.

▶ Any piece we choose, bottoms in particular, must have drape and stretch for a skimming (never tight or clingy) fit. As you have probably experienced, the difference in fabrics that drape over your curves, mold and hold you in slightly, versus stiff fabrics that bunch and create sharp horizontal creases is considerable.

▶ We'll choose interesting layers, jackets and coats in soft textures, vertical patterns and prints, that define a look—and your curves— layered over monochromatic and tonal pieces for the almighty unbroken line. Choosing tops simply to cover your bottom is not the intent here. This is important. Ill-fitting jackets and tops pulled over a full bottom act as a spotlight rather than a camouflage. We're after the critical combination of skimming layers in compatible lengths designed in fabrics that drape.

▶ We *will* choose horizontal stripes for your tops— paying attention to how the stripes are spaced. Thin horizontal lines that are narrowly spaced actually lengthen your line. They create an optical illusion that draws the eye up and down much as a vertical line does.

We'll leave these things on the rack:

▶ Oversized T-shirts and camp shirts—in fact, just about anything oversized. We're looking for a sensuous drape that smoothes over—never hides—your shape or swamps your shoulder line.

▶ Any peg top style pants with thick elastic waists and jeans with pleated waists, baggy legs, and tapered ankles. Ditto stirrups and leggings. These shapes not only look dated, the design principle at work here is just plain wrong. Narrowing the line at the ankle accentuates a full bottom and hips. We can find far more flattering options for you. We're looking for skimming (never tight) cuts that create your longest-looking body line in *current* shapes.

Some of what I will advise for you may fly in the face of the advice you've received your entire life on dressing for your size. Again, suspend what you think you know and keep an open mind. I'll recommend combinations of proportions that I have found (through considerable trial and error in the dressing room) will create flattering silhouettes.

specific tips for petites

For all body types 5′4″ and under.

▶ Shop in the petites department (and at specialty stores that offer petite lengths in pants, specifically). The proportions have been worked out for you. Nothing is tougher, and usually less successful, than trying to alter missy or full-fashion sizes that have been proportioned for an average height range. Shortening things alone doesn't do the trick. Details like pockets, buttons, and pant rises never end up in the right place.

▶ Choose narrow silhouettes, worn close to the body, in fabrics with soft drape. Stiff fabrics will give you a boxy line.

▶ Avoid contrasting colors between your tops and bottoms. Monochromatic and tonal combinations are the best way to achieve an unbroken, vertical line. Add interest to monochromatic combinations with different fabrics and textures, top and bottom.

▶ When you choose prints or pattern, look for vertically designed, smaller-scaled graphics in black and white for example, rather than oversized or exploded multicolored prints. Wear your prints on the top to draw the eye upward.

▶ Look for details that create vertical lines on the body like seaming, single-breasted jackets and coats; zip-front jackets. Horizontal lines will shorten or widen the appearance of your body. This

Sarong: At low waist; soft diagonal drape across your belly and hips; worn from knee length to just above the ankle for type A girls of medium to tall height.

> **TIP:** Choose dark neutral bottoms in fabrics like superfine wools, midweight matte jersey, washed silks (circle and A-line) and firm wool, cotton twill (straight styles). Wear enough heel height to lengthen the look of your legs. Knee-high boots and pumps with a low vamp will slim your ankles and calves.

> **AVOID:** Bells and whistles on your bottoms. Appliques (unless they are monochromatic or tonal, spare, and placed on the diagonal), fussy horizontal trims. Oversized prints; plaids; horizontal pattern; will draw the eye to your lower body. *Keep your choices simple and save the visual interest for your tops.*

Your Tops

Fitted, tailored shirts: Define the shape of your torso in cotton, linen, and silk, with features like princess seams and darts that are built in to create shape and avoid a boxy line. You can pull off things like lace, breast pockets, shirring, ruching, trims—all details that draw the eye upward and add a subtle volume to your shoulders and upper body.

Boat neck, ballet neck, square neck: In torso skimming, lightweight knits. A horizontal line at your neck will visually widen your shoulders; horizontal or chevron stripes (stripes meeting at a central point forming an inverted **V**) will add width to your torso and a visual balance for your bottom.

Necklines at midchest to throat: V-necks, ovals, sweetheart necks, crewnecks, mandarin collars, and T-necks draw the eye upward. Choose skimming fit, hitting at hipbone length.

Wrap tops: Should accentuate your waist; lie smooth against your torso. A good style for subtle trims, pattern, hitting at high-hip to hipbone length and worn with smooth-topped skirts and pants.

Banded tops: Knit banding at the bottom of a button-front shirt for a blouson effect to add a little volume to your upper body, hitting at low waist to high hip and worn with a smooth-topped bottom.

Small-scale prints/graphic pattern: Liberty florals; paisleys, pin dots; gingham checks; won't overwhelm your small torso. Chevron stripes and French sailor stripes add subtle volume

Shoulder treatments: Epaulettes, pin-tucking, piping; shirring, well-placed details like diagonal or horizontal button treatments, flowers, soft bows, appliqués will all add subtle volume to your shoulder line.

Cape sleeves: This short sleeve style has no armhole seam that ends at your upper arm creating the illusion of a broader shoulder line. Works for small, toned upper arms.

Halters/camisoles: Fine if your shoulders are not sloped or significantly narrower than your lower body. If they are very narrow, opt for sleeveless styles that create a line through the middle of your shoulder blades so they look broader.

TIP: In general, your tops should hit you at your hipbone to keep your torso long-looking, while avoiding a line across the broadest part of your backside for the smoothest blending of your tops and bottoms.

AVOID: Any top that hits you at your navel or above; it will visually cut your body in half and accentuate the proportionate difference between your upper and lower body.

Your Jackets and Coats

Any jacket you choose should hit you either at your high hip to hipbone if worn with smooth, draped skirts and smooth topped pants or should hit just below your bottom to fingertip length. Avoid any jacket that hits your low hip—visually your widest point.

Nipped waist: Waist definition and a torso-skimming fit create a shapely line. Look for slightly fitted styles with vertical seaming through the torso; set-in sleeves with a small shoulder pad. Wear this cut at high hip to hipbone length with trousers or a soft, draped skirt.

Belted: Think cardigan with a sash tie. This shape works in soft fabrics, midweight knits, at hipbone length. Ideal with your soft skirts.

Bombers and blousons: Slightly bloused with a banded bottom sitting at low waist to high hip; worn with smooth-topped skirts.

Chanel jacket: Only slightly boxy; close to the body fit, worn unbuttoned over a fitted T-shirt or lightweight sweater, both hittting at high hip to hipbone.

Jeans jacket: Close fitting; vertical seams for shape; cropped to hit your waist or low waist; to wear with smooth cotton skirts, for example. Or try a nipped-waist jacket with lapels, button front, and torso seaming, that hits at your high hip worn with your smooth-topped straight pants.

AVOID: The traditional boxy style—it will hide your torso and give you a blocky line as the eye moves up and down.

A-line coat: Narrow or set-in shoulders flaring slightly from under the arms to the hem in an A-line shape; worn at knee length; single or double breasted.

Trench and military styles: Wide lapel, single or double-breasted style, epaulettes, belted waist and an A-line drape from waist to hem.

Princess: A fitted coat constructed of wide panels that flare at the hem, worn at knee length to midcalf, single-breasted.

TIP: To extend your shoulder line subtly for balance and definition, have a tailor put a thin *dolman* shoulder pad into any tailored jacket or coat that doesn't have them already. Usually, just a little extra definition provides a natural and current-looking silhouette.

Your Dresses

Empire: Your best dress silhouette with its emphasis on the upper body, a feminine neckline, and décolletage easing into a fuller shape that smoothes over your hips, bottom, and thighs. Look for wide oval, square, or V necklines at midchest, which draw the eye upward and embellishments on the bodice like pleating, ruching, horizontal neck trims. Wear at knee length with a leg-lengthening metallic sandal, a high heel with a low vamp, or with calf-slimming, high-heeled boots. *An ideal style to own in black.*

Wrap dresses: Best in solids or tonal prints with a pattern that is consistent in size and spacing overall to achieve visual balance between your upper and lower body. Make sure that the skirt has an A-line construction and that the fabric, matte jersey for example, has enough weight to drape softly around your hips and bottom.

type

A looks

you have

- Small to medium frame
- Average to full bust
- Small to average, defined waistline
- Curvy hips
- Round, average to full bottom
- Shapely legs

our plan

Your well-proportioned line of shoulders in balance with your hips, a shapely bust, defined waistline, and good legs, gives you bombshell potential when you're in the mood to dress like an Italian movie star. Smaller-busted type B girls will want to add a molded-cup, slightly padded bra to enhance a curvy silhouette that is in balance with their hips and bottom. We're looking for soft pieces in draped fabrics that accentuate and skim your curves. Your waist should always be a focal point, meaning type B girls should pass on straight full tunic tops and shifts that hide your natural contours. Silhouettes that highlight your waist, worn at knee length to show off your legs, are always on your list. In general, monochromatic and tonal color combinations keep your body line looking long and complement your shape.

Your Pants

Flat-front trouser: Low waist, flat front, hip skimming, easing into a full, straight leg in midweight wools or good quality blends. This clean-line cut with drape flatters your backside (especially if your bottom is curvy and full). Taller girls can pull off wider leg versions. Hem your trousers to wear with heels.

Bootcut: Easy through hips, thigh-skimming with a subtle flare, in lightweight wools; blends; soft suede; matte leathers; dark colors.

Flare: Low waist, flat front, ease through the hip and thigh. A flared hem balances your curves. Best for type B girls of medium to tall height.

AVOID: Very straight, tight fits (cigarette or toreador). They'll make you look wide-hipped and bottom heavy.

body type B

Your Tops

Your tops should be simple or smooth. Look for fabrics that will drape over your curves and follow the natural outline of your shape without clinging to it.

Soft blouse: Simple, softly fitted blouses with seaming, shaping, and darts to complement your bust. Feminine styles with open necklines and soft sleeve treatments won't compete with your curves. When you wear sheer, choose a fitted camisole with a built-in bra construction for a sleek line underneath.

AVOID: If your bust is fuller, skip breast pockets, pleating, and ruffles. Details that add volume and texture over your bust will look fussy. Fabrics like cotton voile, washed silk, and stretch silk chiffon minus the bells and whistles work well.

Blouson: Softly bloused and gathered in a band and hitting at the low waist has the same effect of blousing a shirt slightly over a belt. Flattering for any bust. Wear with your bias or straight skirts or a smooth-waisted trouser.

Wrap tops: A deep V crossover in matte jersey; flat, fine-gauge sweater knits, midweight cotton knits.

Halters: A plunging V front and a focus on the décolletage that you can pull off in firm matte jersey and knits, worn with bias or circle skirts or your trousers for day-into-evening options.

T-shirts: Tight baby tees with cap sleeves are not your best look. Opt for soft, skimming cotton in lengths that hit your high hip to hipbone for the most flattering line. Tanks shouldn't have a sprayed-on quality. Full busts should choose cotton or jersey knits over thin rib knits.

Your Jackets and Coats

Nipped waist: Will reinforce a waist-defining line; single breasted, notched collar, a single button at or just below the waist. One to three button styles define the silhouette worn at high hip to hip bone. Look for variations on this style in denim as an alternative to a classic jean jacket.

Jeans jacket: The traditional cut of this staple is not your best bet. Look for riffs on the style in soft washed denim, corduroy, cotton twill in cuts with a nip at the waist, shaped vertical seams, hitting at hip bone to high hip. Don't hide your shape under a boxy cut.

Belted: One of your best choices with its emphasis on your waist. Worn at high hip to hip bone with smooth skirts and pants. Girls with fuller booties should choose just below the bottom lengths to wear with jeans. Look for simple styling. Safari or military details like pockets at breast and hips can be too busy for the soft contours of most type B girls. Cashmere and wool blends, lightweight wool, supple suede or soft, low-sheen leathers, minimally detailed, enhance the line.

Cardigan: Slightly fitted in simple, minimally textured or flat wools for flattering drape, worn at high hip to hipbone length with your full trousers, pencil skirts.

Wrap coat: No buttons, shawl or small-notch collar, wrapped with a sash tie and worn at knee length.

Classic, single breasted coat: Follow same fit principles as your nipped-waist jacket.

avoid

AVOID: Any fabrics that add bulk and hide your curves. Remember to look for drape. Skins like shearling or leather should be supple, quilted styles and have a skimming fit or a subtly shaped construction. Pass on double-breasted and boxy, oversized blazers or jackets. They'll hide your waist and give you a blocky line.

Your Dresses

Nipped-waist sheath: Torso skimming and subtle shaping at waist give definition to this straight construction worn at knee length.

Tank dress: Body conscious with clean lines that skim your curves, knee length to show off your legs. Deep V; oval necklines flatter your bust. A loose belt or sash (resting at low waist) suggests your waistline; eases over a fuller bust.

Bias: Diagonal cuts with plenty of drape and halter, Hollywood, or tank necklines; center-front and center-back seams for a sleek, vertical line in matte jersey; silks, draped lightweight wools; knits worn at knee length to just above the ankle.

Wrap dress: A perennial favorite for shapely girls, a deep V neckline and asymmetric drape make this a sure thing for a smooth, sexy silhouette that accentuates your waist and legs.

Strapless: If you have a very full bust, look for styles with boning and support built in, a defined waist, vertical seams through the torso for shape; a pencil or circle skirt silhouette worn at knee length.

type

Blooks

you have

- Average to broad shoulders (wider than your hips)
- Medium to very full bust line
- Straight, short-to-average waist
- Narrow hips
- Often, a flat rather than rounded bottom
- Slim legs

our plan

Like a lot of models, you have strong shoulders, narrow hips, and slim legs, which give you choice and versatility. Our balancing act for most type C girls in clothing shapes and proportions is to choose what will create a longer-looking middle if your bust and torso are full or if you have a short waist. If you are a thin type C and your figure is boyish, we'll look for shapes and details that create definition for your waist. If you have broad shoulders, we'll stay clear of styles that exaggerate their width in relation to your narrow lower body. Solid colors above your waist keep your torso slimmer and longer looking and your shoulders softer-looking. Let it rip on the bottom however. Your narrow hips let you choose from all kinds of trends, patterns, and details.

Your Pants

Really, it's your choice. With your narrow hips and slim legs, there are few pant shapes or lengths that you can't wear (what's that like?). Hip huggers to Hepburn trousers, cropped to floor grazing, narrow to wider legs, you can carry them off, depending on your height. Wear them from low waist to hipbone. You can finesse cuts

> **TIP:** If you have a short waist (especially if your middle is full and you have a low bust line) pass on high-waist pants. They'll cut your body line in half, shortening the appearance of your upper body and exaggerating the width of your shoulders in relation to your lower body.

body type c

like harem pants, gauchos, knickers, pedal pushers, and all matter of patch and cargo pockets, zippers, ties and straps; in short, the bells and whistles in any season.

Jeans: Again, take your pick. From old-school Levis 501s to the jeans du jour, you can pretty much wear them all.

> **TIP:** If your bottom is flat, watch out for very low rises, which will make it appear more so by exaggerating the straight line from your torso into your hips and bottom. Instead, try them a little higher on your hip with a medium-wide, contoured belt to create the illusion of curvier, rounder hips and butt.

Capris/crops: Take your pick of fabrics, patterns, and varying lengths from midcalf to just above the ankle.

Shorts: Again, with your narrow lower body and slim legs you can wear most any length. Petites and shorter girls look great in leg-lengthening short shorts (hot pants that hit anywhere from 3″ to 5″). Medium to tall type C girls look especially great in knee-length pedal pushers. Be sure to keep your overall line slim and long-looking with skimming (never oversized) tops at hipbone length.

> **TIP:** Unless you're Outward Bound, no chunky workout sneakers with your shorts. Depending upon your destination, opt instead for a sleek, flat sandal or an old-school, simple sneaker.

Your Skirts

Your stylist loves a little shape and drape in skirts for you. At knee length, in general, constructions that create the illusion of a little curviness, and details like contoured waistbands, pockets at your front and back at hip level that add a slight volume to your hips, will help balance your overall body line, especially when worn at the low waist.

Torso skirts: A style that has soft pleating, gathering, or tiers attached to a smooth yoke that falls from your waist to your hips. This is your stylist's first choice for type C girls.

Godet: Triangular pieces of fabric are inserted upward at the hemline for shape.

Circle/flare: Skims over hips and a wide, full hem.

Pencil: No waistband, skimming fit and a slight tapering at hemline worn at just below the knee length with high heels to accentuate your legs.

Trouser: Sitting at low waist to high hip; a contoured waistband for shape through the hip, worn just above to just below the knee.

A-line: In drapey and firm fabrics.

Stitch-down pleats/broomstick: In soft cotton voile, washed silk, lightweight wool.

Sarong: From short to ankle length, fabric wrapped and draped around your hips or designed to simulate the look, adds subtle volume; the illusion of curve to your hips.

Bias: Worn from knee length to just-above-the-ankle length (if you are medium height to tall). Inspect your rear view however; if your booty runs to the flatter end of the spectrum, make this your last choice.

TIP: Plaids cut on the horizontal (think kilts) or on the bias/diagonal will flatter you but make sure any plaid you choose matches perfectly at the seams. You can pull off mid-to-large scale prints and patterns. Horizontal embellishments and border trims at the hemline will spotlight your legs.

AVOID: Full pleats gathered at the natural waist, like dirndls. This style will appear to cut you in half, shortening the appearance of your torso and exaggerating your upper body.

Your Tops

Tailored shirts: A natural choice for your angular shape. The shapes you choose, from tapered to a slightly fuller cut, depend on the length and width of your torso and the fullness of your bust. Good in crisp cotton, stretch cotton poplin with a contoured, finished shirttail, soft silk knit jerseys, matte jersey, and soft suede. A classic combination for type C girls: a tailored shirt hitting from high hip to just below the bottom length, untucked over slim pants.

TIP: If you have a short waist, opt for shirts that you can wear untucked at hipbone length, paired with smooth waistlines. Treatments like ruching along the front placket of a button front shirt minimize a full bust and torso.

V-necks, U-necks: From midchest to cleavage will create a slimming, lengthening vertical line from your face and neck into your torso, worn at hipbone length. Cashmere, merino knits, and cotton interlock with stretch are all good fabric choices. If you have a full bust (and especially if you have a short waist) choose necklines at midchest or higher so that your upper body looks longer, creating a focal point above your bust/torso. For thin type C's look for these necklines in sweaters and cotton tops that have a small belt, or add a thin belt or ribbon tie to create a little waist definition. Try with your pencil or flared skirts to create a curvy illusion.

V-neck cardigan sweater: Unbuttoned, hitting at hip length. Your shoulders give this timeless option an instant line. This linear silhouette with drape over your torso and bust is especially important if you have a short waist. Layering, with something very feminine underneath like a silk camisole, offers soft, skimming definition—a natural paired with your pencil skirt.

Surplice tops: Work for you in fabrics that drape, like silk knits, stretch silk, midweight matte jerseys, and viscose worn at high hip to hipbone length to avoid a short-waisted look. Slimming side-ruched styles, a low **V** neckline, and the diagonal drape across the torso suggest a longer waistline. A feminine top with smooth, flared skirts.

Blouson: Drapes over and minimizes a full middle and bust. A wide neckline sliding off a shoulder, hitting your hips creates a lengthening line. Ideal paired with smooth topped, slim pants or a pencil skirt.

TIP: Look for styles with soft sleeve treatments that de-emphasize your shoulders like raglan, kimono, and dropped shoulder; worn hip length with smooth bottoms.

Sleeveless: To keep your shoulder line in balance with your lower body in slim bottoms, look for tanks with wider straps that meet or come close to the edge of your shoulders with U- or V-necks. Spaghetti straps on tanks or camisole dress tops are best balanced by skirts with a bit of volume and drape; very broad shoulders, watch out for halter necklines, as the placement of the straps will visually cut into your shoulders, creating a diagonal line that will exaggerate their width.

AVOID: The widening effect of horizontal lines at your shoulders such as set-in, puffed, or gathered sleeves, boat necks, square necks, epaulettes, horizontal piping, appliqués, and stripes—all details that will exaggerate the width of your shoulders in relation to your lower body.

Your Jackets and Coats

Blazer: Look for styles with soft, natural shoulders and a high cut arm which will create the illusion of a longer torso by drawing the eye upward; single breasted; small lapels; hitting from high hip to low hip depending on the style.

TIP: Look for a *low stance*—a tailoring term that refers to the point where the buttons and the lapels meet and the V-line that begins at the neck and ends at midchest or cleavage level. A one-button closure at just below your natural waist will draw the eye up and down elongating your upper body line.

Shirt jacket: Create a streamlined vertical line for short waists, full torsos. Look for subtle shaping from vertical seams; small notch or mandarin collars; funnel necks; smooth and undetailed across the breast; pockets; details at hip level.

Belted jacket/coat: Look for styles with a natural shoulder and a belt or tie belt that sits just above the natural waist to just under your bust and hitting at your hipbone for jackets and below the knee for coats. This belt placement will draw the eye upward to create the illusion of a longer waist.

Peplum jacket: A nipped waist and a flared hemline add volume at your hips and the illusion of a curvier lower body. Best for slim type C's worn at high hip to hipbone length with a pencil skirt to accentuate the curvy silhouette.

Classic coat: There are always updated takes on this slightly A-line, well-cut staple. From cashmere to cotton canvas this construction is ideal for your silhouette, as your strong shoulders give the shape a defined line, worn at knee length.

Pea coat: Semifitted, double-breasted; a structured notch collar worn at high hip with slim skirts or hip length to a just-below-your-bottom length for pants.

Cardigan coat: Collarless with a straight-lined construction, worn from high hip to knee length in soft supple fabrics like coatweight sweater knits, cashmere, double-faced/reversible wools, supple leather, and soft suede to keep the look fluid and avoid a boxy look. A skimming silhouette for type C girls who are fuller through the torso.

Wrap jacket or coat: Best for average-length torsos in lightweight wools, cashmere-wool blends, heavyweight sweater knits. If you are short-waisted, wear the sash belt at your low waist to keep your torso line looking long. Lower belt loops if necessary.

Trench coats: Same principle as above—look for a modern take on the silhouette, minus the traditional trappings like epaulettes, large lapels, or right shoulder flap, that will exaggerate your shoulders. Same advice as above for the placement of your belt.

AVOID: If you have a full bust, pass on prominent breast pockets on your jackets and coats. If your shoulders are broad, bypass wide lapels as well as any set-in or puffed sleeves, which will exaggerate their width in relation to your lower body. All sleeve seams should hit the outer edge of your shoulders. Remove any shoulder pads. Mother Nature has you covered.

Your Dresses

Shift: Semifitted through the waist or straight if you have a fuller bust and torso. Ideal worn at knee length with high heels to create a line that emphasizes your legs. A straight shape can also work with a sash tied loosely at your high hip. Look for soft, draped fabrics like jersey and silk. Day or evening, look for variations on this shape with current sleeve treatments and deep **V** or **U** necklines that tweak the basic construction. Have one in black at all times.

Tunic: You are the girl who looks great in a tunic with flat sandals and a whole lot of your slim legs.

Torso dress: A silhouette that follows the line of the body to the hips where the skirt is attached. Look for thin belts, ribbon ties at the waist. An illusory, lengthening torso line for average and short-waisted type C girls and a skirt cut to add curve at the hip (like your torso skirt).

Strapless: Slim and straight constructed with a pencil skirt or gored skirt; a thin belt resting at the waist installs an illusory curviness. A wider belt or obi sash attached to a flared skirt with drape is also a good silhouette. A fuller shape at the hemline provides a graceful balance for broad-shouldered type C girls.

Shirt or coat dress: A slightly fitted or straight construction, a small shirt collar or small lapels, button front, worn at knee length to show off your legs with a pair of heels or high-heeled boots. Good in wool jersey, silk, soft suede, as well as classic cotton sateen.

A-line: Semifitted through torso and widening gradually to hemline; works in soft fabrics.

Wrap dress: For girls with average-length waists since the placement of the tie will emphasize a short waist. A good variation on this theme for short-waisted girls is a surplice style, side ruched; a low V neckline and diagonal drape across the torso suggest a longer waistline.

Bathrobe: Collarless with a slightly dropped shoulder, a low V neckline, wrapping with a self-tied sash. Draped and sexy in sweater knits, jersey, or silk.

Kimono: Softly draped, wraparound construction made with kimono sleeves. Look for current takes with slim skirts, closing with a sash tie—good over pants.

TIP: Medium to tall type C girls can pull off the dress over slim pants combo. Try this look with your tunic, bathrobe, or kimono styles in lightweight or sheer fabrics and either flat sandals or very high heels for evening.

type

looks

you have

- Narrow or sloping shoulders
- Small to medium bust (proportionate to your shoulders)
- Full waist
- Wide hips
- Very full thighs and calves

our plan

We'll create a balanced body line by choosing tops that create a focal point above your waist and broaden the appearance of your shoulder line, paired with simple, draped bottoms that smooth and ease over the curves of your lower body. Critical for all your separates: a smooth meeting point (without pulling, clinging, or bunching) between your tops and bottoms.

Your Pants

Your best choices will have either a minimal waistband or no waistband, a side or front fly zip, worn at your natural waist. Choose styles that have ease through the leg in straight or subtly flared styles. Pass on anything highwaisted, meaning above your natural waist. This will shorten the appearance of your torso. Avoid pleats, anything with a tapered ankle. No leggings.

Straight trouser: Fullness through the seat and legs is always essential for pants that will flatter you. One shape that best accomplishes this is a trouser which has a straight full leg to streamline your lower body. Try this style worn right at your navel—no higher—for the illusion of a longer torso. Suits any type D.

> **TIP:** This shape should always be constructed from fabrics with a firm enough hand like lightweight seasonless wools, wool crepe, firm cotton that falls without cling. If pants do not have a full or partial lining to the knee, have one put in by a tailor (*see* chapter 5) or buy a pant liner or lower-body shaper in the lingerie department. For jerseys and knits, always choose a lower-body shaper to smooth out and flatter your bottom line. More on this in chapter 6.

body type D

Wide-leg trouser: Flat front, at your natural waist (to elongate the look of your torso); no waistband or a very thin waistband with front and back darts for shape; a side or front zipper and elastic if needed, placed subtly at the back. The shaping and clean finish provided by the darts and a full leg will smooth over your abdomen and hips and provide a flattering line from your seat down over your thighs. A slight flare at the hem provides modern-looking hip balance. Hem to wear with at least a 1½ inch heel to elongate your lower body line and wear your pants long enough to brush the top of your shoe. Again, unlined pants need the visual smoothing of a lining or foundation garment. Best for medium height to tall type D girls.

Yoga/pajama: Pull-on styles that don't narrow at the ankle and are best constructed in fabrics like heavy matte jersey, midweight knits, firm linens. Choose versions in fabrics with enough substance so that they drape rather than droop or cling, worn in shades monochromatically or tonally matched with your top. In lightweight, gauzy fabrics this is a flattering shorts alternative for hot weather.

Jeans: Look for a *contoured* waist, meaning the waistline rises slightly higher in the back than in the front. Dark indigo or black stretch denim and a full leg with a slightly flared hem will visually balance your hips. Skimming, never tight, worn at your natural waist. For a sleek variation on the theme, look for versions of your straight trouser in washed dark stretch indigo or black denim. Again, a full straight leg lengthens your line, skimming your hips for a proportionate-looking balance. Try styles with no waistband when you find them to provide the smooth finish you need under layering pieces. Wear with a jacket that falls at your high hip or just below your bottom, or a fingertip length jacket unbuttoned over a skimming tee at roughly the same length. Keep your colors top and bottom tonal or monochromatic. Hem your jeans to wear with at least a 1½ inch heel. As above, wear with a sleek, tonal boot, for example, to elongate the line.

AVOID: Any small or elaborately detailed back pockets along with engineered fading or whiskering and cargo styling in general. Keep your jeans simple, long, dark, and minimally detailed and they'll work with and not against your curves.

Your Skirts

Your best skirt shapes will fit you closely at the waist and either ease over your hips or drape softly around them. Worn at just below the knee, with a leg-lengthening monochromatic match of your skirt, hosiery, and high heels or knee-high stretch leather boots, you can create a longer, leaner look for your legs. Your skirts are the linchpin of your wardrobe—match them monochromatically with tops of the same fabric like matte jersey for example, for day and night rather than struggling with dresses that don't fit both your upper and lower body.

Gored skirt: My favorite for you, as its construction of wide panels sewn together for a smoothing drape works with your curves. Just below the knee to the length that flatters you best, worn with a top or jacket that hits your high hip; with knee-high stretch leather boots, for one example; this skirt silhouette complements your shape and looks current.

Flared: A variation on the gored construction—a subtle A-line with center seams front and back in draped fabrics only. This is a great shape worn from a just-below-the-knee length to just above the ankle with a match of hosiery or tights and shoes or stretch boots; high heel sandals for knee-length skirts and above the ankle lengths alike.

Stitch-down pleats: In lightweight, soft fabrics or matte jersey worn just below the knee for graceful movement and a minimizing drape. Again, combine with monochromatic or tonal tops that hit your high hip. A variation on the drape and textural illusion of pleats is a **broomstick** skirt with vertical ridges and wrinkles in soft gauzy fabrics. A skimming hot-weather alternative to shorts or capris.

Straight skirt: Critical to the construction: very soft, small gathers in a thin waistband to provide shape and avoid pulling across your backside; constructed from medium-firm fabrics. Wear at just below the knee with a monochromatic match of your skirt, stockings, and sleek, low vamp pumps or stretch leather boots. Best for medium height to tall type D girls.

AVOID: Petites and shorter than average type D girls should stay clear of all stick-straight, ankle-length, pull-on skirts. You will most often find these in lightweight jersey which will mold to your backside and the silhouette (or lack of one) will visually weigh you down. Opt instead for draped, fluid styles that widen subtly at the hemline to balance and compliment your curves and that fall at above ankle length.

Your Tops

The tops you choose should sit at your low waist to high hip to avoid any pulling across your lower hips and bottom (and riding up). Long tunic tops that cover your backside may be too large for your shoulderline and will emphasize the proportional difference between your upper and lower body. Choose set-in sleeves to widen the appearance of your shoulder line and make sure that the armhole is full enough to avoid any pulling across your bust. Unless a shoulder pad is thin and natural-looking, remove and replace it with a dolman pad (*see* chapter 6 for this and other options).

Look for necklines like boat or ballet, sweetheart, U- and V-necks, mock necks. For evening, a top with a combination of a matte torso construction and sheer illusion sleeves for example, creates the appearance of a broader shoulder line and an elongated, sleek torso.

Details like textures, subtle trims, tonal embroidery, breast pockets, button-front styles, narrow vertical ribs for sweaters, and yoked or smocked shoulder treatments will draw the eye upward to your face and neck. Skimming sleeves at three quarter length are always flattering, as are soft sleeve treatments like cape and kimono.

Banded Bottom: Accentuates your upper body in fabrics like silks, silk knits, or matte jersey for a fluid blouson effect. It is important, however, that the band sit on the top of your high hip so that it doesn't pull across your belly and that the meeting point of your top and bottom is smooth. The slight fullness of this style adds volume to your upper body as a proportion balance for your lower body. Try with straight, full pants or a smooth-topped, flared skirt.

Wrap tops: In midweight stretch, stretch cotton poplin with details like white collar and cuffs, matte jersey, or silk knit. Critical to the look, a top long enough to reach just below your waist with ease so that the top sits smoothly over your waistband. This style looks best with your skirts, and is a shapely alternative to a dress in monochromatic combinations.

Button-front shirts: Look for stretch cotton poplin and details like ruching along the front placket to add volume to your bust. Styles that are cut with a rounded shirttail or with a slit at each side of the hem, should hit your low waist to high hip to avoid any pulling across your hips or bottom. The intent is that, with a subtle dolman shoulder pad, the top fits at the shoulders, skims your body, and just covers the waistband of your straight or wide-leg pants or the smooth top of a skirt.

TIP: Remember, in any structured tops try extending your shoulder line subtly with a thin shoulder pad. If your shoulders slope forward, try shifting the pad back slightly, and extending the blunt edge about a half inch past your shoulder bones (*see* chapter 6).

Your Jackets and Coats

The biggest fit dilemma that a type D girl encounters in jackets and coats is the balance needed between what fits her top and what will smooth over her bottom.

Cropped Jackets: Help type D girls avoid the struggle with hips and bottom. Combined with a smooth skirt or your straight pants, a cropped jacket that hits just below your waist to your high hip creates an elongating line and a smooth meeting point between jacket and bottom. Look for styles with wide lapels; shawl collars that broaden the line of your shoulders. Seaming or *contouring* (meaning cut slightly longer in the front), finished with a rounded shirttail hem for example, will smooth over your abdomen and create the illusion of a longer upper body. The goal is to fit your shoulders and torso and to avoid swamping yourself in excess fabric to accommodate your lower body. When necessary, extend your shoulder line with a very thin dolman pad for the illusion of broader shoulders (*see* chapter 6).

Jeans jacket: In washed denim or stretch corduroy for example. Same fit and shape principles as your cropped style. Avoid any cut that is boxy and hits below your high hip.

Seamed fit and flare coat: This can be a very successful silhouette. Look for a coat that is comfortably fitted over your upper body, ideally with an armhole that is placed just outside your natural shoulder line. The coat should gradually flare to the hemline. Look closely at how the coat is constructed. What keeps this style from looking too stiff in wool is well-placed seaming to install shape. For instance, a horizontal empire seam below the breast that visually divides the top from the bottom can be flattering. Vertical panels install ease so that the shape will drape over your curves rather than standing away from the body in a stiff A-line. Wear just below the knee to low calf. A monochromatic match of a stretch leather boot or stocking and shoe will reinforce a long-looking line.

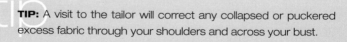

TIP: A visit to the tailor will correct any collapsed or puckered excess fabric through your shoulders and across your bust.

Swing coats: For sweater coats and other layering pieces, this style looks most modern in flat or vertically textured, midweight knits like merino, cashmere, or matte jersey. Skip details like lapels or buttons and opt for vertical border trim like leather piping or a subtle fringe trim, for example. A fingertip-length sweater coat in a dark or rich color is classically chic and immune to trends. For outerwear, choose cashmere; supple wool blends that are soft and drape in styles with simple and tonal buttons; closures; vertical trims.

Your Dresses

In general, I recommend that type D girls concentrate on finding separates that create the look of a flattering dress and avoid the difficulty of finding one piece that balances your top and bottom. A natural choice for fabrics here: midweight matte jersey with substantial drape; lined stretch silks. Choose monochromatic matches of deep, rich colors along with classics like black or navy. Try midsized patterns that are tonal and uniformly spaced. Here are your two best bets for balanced fit off the rack.

TIP: Buy any dress you love one size larger and have a tailor alter the top to achieve the balance needed between your upper and lower body (*see* chapter 5).

Empire: Fitted over your bust and falling into very soft gathers and a gradually flaring hem. Look for boat necklines; feminine shapes like a deep U or ballet neck; full sleeve treatments that extend your shoulder line like cape or kimono, in smooth, draped fabrics. For evening, bodice embellishments like tonal embroidery, shirring, and ruching will draw the eye upwards.

Wrap dresses: In firm-weight jerseys. Look for a top that fits you like a softly draped (not tight) wrap shirt with either an A-line or circle skirt construction on the bottom that falls just below the knee to above the ankle with a monochromatic match of shoes and stockings, stretch boots, or bronzed legs and a nude or metallic sandal to keep that leg line looking long.

type

D looks

you have

- Full, round neck
- Average to broad shoulders and a wide, often rounded, back
- Full, rounded bust
- Full, defined waist
- Hips in proportion with your shoulders
- Shapely legs

our plan

We'll choose shapes that skim your torso with soft drape to streamline the appearance of your upper body. We're looking for open necklines that draw the eye up and down, and create a focus from your neck to your shoulders and décolletage. We'll create an additional focal point at your legs with body-conscious shapes and at-the-knee lengths. We'll keep your pants essentially straight and tailored.

Your Pants

You have shapely hips and legs so pants are a great option for you. Good choices will have no waistband and a side or back zip, worn at, or just below, your natural waistline. Choose straight or subtly flared styles that have ease through the leg. Watch out for anything highwaisted, however; pass on pleats and tapered ankles. Choose dark to midtone colors.

Straight Trouser: Flat front, sitting at your navel (to elongate the look of your torso); no waistband or a minimal waistband; front and back darts for shape and ease; side or front zipper and elastic only if needed (and placed subtly at the back of the waist only). A full leg with drape creates a graceful line. If pants are unlined, either have a lining put in by a tailor (*see* chapter 5) or choose a pant liner or lower-body smoother in the lingerie department to assure a smooth line (*see* chapter 6).

Bootcut: A full-cut leg; subtle widening at hem offers flattering hip balance in fabrics that drape like lightweight stretch wools; stretch narrow wale corduroy; hemmed to wear with heels.

body type E

Yoga/pajama: Drawstring, pull-on styles with a straight, full leg that doesn't narrow at the ankle. Choose fabrics like midweight matte jersey that drape rather than cling. Wear shades monochromatically or tonally matched with your top. Again, avoid those allover, bunchy elastic waists.

Jeans: Look for jeans with the same silhouette as your straight pants, like a relaxed bootcut. Slight width at the hem creates hip balance and a long-looking lower body. Choose dark stretch denim and, whenever you spot a style with no waistband or back pockets, give it a try. Taller type E girls should also try styles with a flare hem. Pass on styles with tricky engineered fading or whiskering. Wear your jeans at your low waist (belly button) and long enough for at least a 1½ inch heel or higher.

Capris/crops: In firm (not stiff) cottons with shape worn from just above the ankle to low calf. Choose rich colors; prints should be midsized and tonal. Key to the look: T-shirts; tailored shirts that skim at high hip or just below your bottom.

Shorts: Pedal pushers at just below the knee and cut with the same ease as your straight pant, no waistband or minimal waistband, firm cottons like stretch twill. Washable silks work for shorts at just above your knee that function as a split skirt.

TIP: To avoid a Girl-Scout-in-search-of-a-merit-badge look in your cropped pants or shorts—no chunky workout sneakers! Depending upon your destination, opt instead for a sleek, flat sandal; an old-school, simple trainer.

Your Skirts

Straight: Small waistband with slight gathers, at knee length to accentuate your legs. You can handle vertical patterns that draw the eye to your shapely hips and legs. Best-bet fabrics: heavyweight jersey, lightweight wool with stretch, firm cottons like stretch twill, subtle texture like stretch Ultrasuede.

Trouser skirt: Another good construction to emphasize your shapely lower body. Pair this with a shirt-styled jacket to continue the long, lean line and to smooth over your middle. Look for fabrics like lightweight stretch wool or stretch cotton twill.

Pencil: Straight and tapering at the knee. Ideal in lightweight stretch wool; wool jersey; worn at just below the knee length with high heels. Try this style with a torso-skimming V-neck top that falls at your high hip.

Thin, stitch down pleats: In lightweight silks; cottons; knits worn at knee length with a top that hits from high hip or just below your bottom for a streamlined effect.

Gored: A construction of vertical panels sewn together for a sensuous drape will skim over your curves. Works well at knee length to low calf for taller type E girls. Try with a skimming, midweight jersey top that falls at hipbone length or just below your bottom.

Bias: Emphasizes a curvy drape for your lower body. Look for styles with panels sewn on the diagonal to visually reinforce the shape. Check your bottom line carefully, however. If your butt looks flat or square, hang the skirt back on the rack. A good style for asymmetric hemlines that draw the eye to your legs.

TIP: If your skirts tend to hang lower in the front and higher in the back it means that your waistline is sloped. On the set I've often rolled the waistband in the front to correct the problem. This works in a pinch if you cover the waistband with a top or soft sash belt (layered with a jacket) but this is best solved at the tailor.

Your Tops

We're looking for drape to work with your voluptuous upper body. We'll pass on anything clingy; too fitted. Silks, matte jerseys and merino knits are made for you. Avoid tops and full shirts (like camp shirts) that are so oversized that the shoulder seam hangs somewhere on your upper arm. Bypass any tailored top that doesn't meet the edge of your shoulders to avoid a sloppy line.

There are two ways you can go with the proportion you choose on top. We'll de-emphasize a full middle with what is traditionally known as shirt styling. A straight-cut shirt (or jacket) at just below your bottom to fingertip length worn open over skimming monochromatic or tonal underpinnings creates the almighty, unbroken line.

Tops with open oval, V, asymmetric necklines, and an easy body-skimming fit look great ending from your high hip or just below your bottom. Choose full armholes and sleeve treatments that are not constructed with a set-in shoulder seam. This assures a smooth, skimming fit across your upper arms; ease over your bust. Look for any of these sleeve styles to create an elongating line.

- **Raglan:** Extends to the neckline and is set in by a diagonal seam from your underarm in the front and back (looks like the sleeve on a baseball jersey).
- **Dolman:** Cut with a very deep armhole so that it looks like a cape from the back and gradually narrows to a fitted wrist (skip this style if you are petite—it will overwhelm your frame).
- **Kimono:** Seams of this wide sleeve run on the outer and inner edge of your arm.

Tailored shirts: Stretch cotton poplin styles; vertical seams for contoured shape and finished shirttails to cover smooth waistbands; contrast collars and cuffs. Wear unbuttoned to midchest for a deep V line that shows a hint of cleavage, layered over a form-fitting camisole

TIP: The less detail on the top the better. We want to create a sleek, uninterrupted line for your upper body. Stick with dark neutrals; rich, deep jewel tones; bright colors that enhance your skin tone. Go easy on ruffles. Choose monochromatic, vertical or diagonal border trim. Embellishments; breast pockets; epaulettes are not best for your bag of tricks. They'll fight your curves.

or tank. Tall type E girls, comb the men's department for tapered cuts in trendy colors and patterns; French cuffs. Any prints should be mid-scale and tonal. Deep V-necks will make your neck appear longer. Small mandarin collars can work; mock necks rather than turtlenecks. Pass on a neckline that makes your neck appear short or heavy. Flipping your shirt or coat collar in the back will lengthen the line of your neck.

Your Jackets and Coats

Shaped Blazer: A skimming shape; vertical seaming to install shape; a nip at the waist; nothing boxy or oversized.

Blouson: Knit banding at the hem of a jacket that falls at hipbone length will define your silhouette in smooth pants, dark jeans, and slim skirts.

Cardigan jacket: Skimming and straight; midthigh to knee length. Whether you choose a vertically knit sweater coat or a topper in suede; soft leather; boiled wool; this style creates an instant vertical line. Ideal for evening in brocade; satin; paired tonally with straight pants; a shift dress.

Wrap coat: In soft fabrics with drape; cashmere; wool blends; soft suede; glove leather, and worn at knee length.

Balmacaan: An easy fit with a raglan sleeve for ease through the bust worn at knee length or longer.

Your Dresses

Shift: In fabrics with stretch and drape; diagonal darts for ease over your bust will skim over your midsection. Look for V and U necklines that accentuate the length of your neck and expose a bit of cleavage for evening; wear with high heels to enhance your leg line. Have one in black.

Shirtwaist: A smooth, undetailed shirt top, unbuttoned to create a low V-neck. Play up those legs with a low vamp pump or a sexy sandal.

Coat: Straight construction; single-breasted styles only; unbuttoned for a low V neckline, at knee length.

Wrap: Best for defined waists. Full mid-section, avoid the fitted (potentially tight) top of this style—it will give you a boxy line. A variation on the theme: styles that have a V neck and ruching from a side seam to create a diagonal drape under your bust; across your abdomen. Create the illusion of a more defined waistline. Ideal day into evening.

type

E looks

you have

- Full neck
- Broad shoulders
- Average to full bust
- Broad rib cage and full torso
- Undefined, full waist (often short)
- Flat bottom
- Slim legs

our plan

We're looking for tops with skimming, straight shapes to elongate the look of your upper body—specifically minimizing the volume of your ribcage and waist. We'll choose bottoms that accentuate your narrow lower body and create a focal point at your legs.

Your Pants

Straight, slim pant: A skimming narrow leg is your very best option, flat front, sits at your natural to low waist (belly button), no waistband or a very thin waistband, and elastic if needed at the back of the waistband only. You can go two ways with fabric. Anything with a little drape like lightweight, stretch wool, or matte jersey will flatter you. Firm fabrics like denim, stretch cotton twill, firm silks, and crisp linens will enhance the silhouette. Look for details like pressed or stitched-down front creases to reinforce the vertical line. A fuller leg in this same shape works for type F girls from medium height to tall.

Keep the top of your pants smooth and uncomplicated. Details like topstitching and pockets near side seams make it difficult for a tailor to take them in through the hips if needed. Your hem length is critical to the overall look. Very straight cuts look best hemmed to brush the top of your shoe—too long and they'll bunch and shorten your leg line. This silhouette looks best with a sleek high-heeled boot with a pointed toe, a shoe with the same line, or a simple sandal that reinforces a sleek line from pant hem down the length of your foot.

Cigarette: In seasonless stretch wools; lined silk; tonal brocades for day to evening. Always have a pair of these in black in your closet.

body type F

Jeans: Since the trickiest thing for you in jeans is good fit through the seat, try a slim shape with the same basic silhouette as your straight pant, which in the world of jeans means bootcut. Try a contoured waistline that sits above your natural waist in the back and dips slightly in the front. A straight line across your backside will emphasize your width there. Install a little curvy illusion and keep the fit as smooth as you can. Any top you wear over your jeans will drape better. No belts. Hem to wear with at least a sleek 1½ inch heel.

Capris/crops: In firm cottons that maintain their shape. Avoid wimpy cottons that droop over your curves. Your slim legs give you flexibility in the lengths you choose, from mid-calf to ankle cropped. Try rich colors and midsized tonal prints. Key to the look, a T-shirt or tailored shirt that skims your body falling from high hip to just below your bottom. Always pass on very oversized tops: they'll give you a blocky line.

Shorts: Bermudas and pedal pushers (for taller type F girls) cut with the same ease as your straight pant; flat front, no waistband or minimal waistband; in washed denims, stretch cotton twill. Soft draped fabric, like washable silk, works for shorts at just above your knee that function as a split skirt. Look for shorter flat-front styles with a built-in tummy control panel. Again, critical to the line, skimming not oversized tops that end from high hip to just below your bottom. Experiment with lengths until you arrive at your most flattering leg line—and overall line—as the proportion of your tops flows into the length of your bottoms to streamline the appearance of your body.

Your Skirts

Straight: Minimal or no waistband sitting at natural or low waist; or a slightly gathered, thin waistband in fabrics that drape like lightweight stretch wool and midweight matte jersey, silk blends, stretch Ultrasuede. Wear at knee length or, if you are petite, raise your hem an inch or two for a longer expanse of leg. Look for details like side slits to accentuate your gams.

Trouser: In firm fabrics with a little stretch for a skimming fit. Look for lightweight stretch denim, stretch cotton twill, and linen blends. The fabric should give you shape without bulk. The waistband should hit your low waist. Make sure any fly front zippers lie flat against your abdomen.

Pencil: No waistband or minimal waistband with small darts for ease worn at natural waist, tapering slightly at the hem for shape, worn at just below the knee. Pair with a torso-skimming tunic top that falls at just below your bottom, and high heels.

Thin, stitch down pleats: Worn at the knee, in crisp cottons or silks, with a top that drapes and skims over your middle and hitting at high hip to just below your bottom.

Flared: Slightly flared, nothing too full or exaggerated, in fabrics that drape only, worn at or just above the knee.

Your Tops

Tunic: This basic shape is the best place to begin for your tops, skimming and straight, in fabrics with drape to smooth over your upper body. Colors, necklines, and sleeve treatments will change the look. This is your ideal silhouette with slim pants and straight skirts alike. Experiment with the length of your tops. A just-below-the-bottom length is flattering and this same cut worn at the high hip can work especially well with your skirts.

> **TIP:** Always have U and V necklines in your closet, along with asymmetric openings cut on the diagonal. Experiment with anything that creates an open, lengthening neckline. Deep side slits at hemlines add to the vertical line. Any pattern you wear over your middle should draw the eye up and down such as prints in mid to large scales, in vertical stripes or chevron stripes (stripes meeting at a central point forming an inverted V), diagonally placed pattern in graphic black and white for example.

For matte jersey, silk, or knit tops look for full armholes and sleeve treatments that are constructed with a shoulder seam that meets the edge of your shoulder for a smooth slimming fit across your upper arms and ease over your bust. Avoid any set-in, gathered, or puffed sleeve treatments. Look for any of these styles to create an elongating line.

- **Dolman:** Cut with a very deep armhole so that it looks like a cape from the back and gradually narrows to a fitted wrist. Look for this treatment in tops that are full through the bust and close fitting at the hips (not for petites; the cut will overwhelm you).
- **Kimono:** Seams of this wide sleeve run on the outer and inner edge of your arm.
- **Raglan:** Sleeve that extends to the neckline and is set in by a diagonal seam from your underarm in the front and back (like the sleeve on a baseball jersey).
- **Illusion:** Full, sheer sleeve combined with a matte jersey or silk body.

Tailored shirts: Look for stretch cotton poplin styles with a straight and skimming cut, vertical seams, and finished, contoured shirttails; details like contrast collars and cuffs. Wear unbuttoned to midchest for a deep-V line that shows some cleavage, layered over a form-fitting camisole or tank with an underwire bra (*see* chapter 6). Tall type F girls, comb the men's department for tapered cuts in trendy colors and subtle patterns, contrast collars and cuffs, and French cuffs. Any prints you choose should be midscale and tonal. The timelessly chic look of a tailored shirt hitting just below your bottom, slim pants, and a kitten heel or higher to raise your body line, is a sure-thing silhouette for type F.

AVOID: Tees and full shirts (camp shirts) that are oversized with shoulder seams that hang somewhere on your upper arm. Bypass any tailored top that falls beyond the edge of your shoulders to avoid an exaggerated or sloppy line. Any neckline that gaps should go straight to the tailor.

Your Jackets and Coats

Blazer: Worn open over tonal, skimming tailored shirts, tees, tanks. A straight cut; single-breasted; small notch collar; a smooth, undetailed shoulder and breast area. Be sure that the shoulder line hits the edge of your natural shoulder or you'll look swamped. Never go oversized on this style. Keep it close to the body, skimming, tailored.

Car coat: Collarless; a skimming or slightly A-line shape in soft fabrics that drape like wools, supple suede, and leather worn from midthigh to knee length. Vertical trims create the illusion of length.

Shirt jacket: Styled with a shirttail hem and side slits, for example, in fabrics ranging from soft suede to soft denim to khaki. A classic layering piece over tonal, skimming tees; tanks that fall 2″ to 3″ above the hem of the jacket to keep the line vertical, unbroken. Looks long and sleek with slim pants.

Pea coat: Easy fit, natural shoulders, double breasted, worn at high hip with knee length skirts to just below your bottom with slim pants.

Cardigan: Collarless and draped silhouette for jackets, coats, sweater coats, worn from midthigh to knee length. Looks great with straight skirts and pants in fabrics like cashmere, suede, supple leather, merino wool, boiled wool, firm silks.

TIP: In any jacket or coat: pockets at hip level only.

Dresses

Shift: Great for you in fabrics with stretch and drape. This straight construction has darts for ease over your bust; will skim over your midsection. Wear at knee length or just above to emphasize your legs. Look for U and V necklines that visually lengthen your neck; wear with at least a 1½ inch heel to elongate your leg line. Look for different sleeve treatments to subtly change the silhouette. Have one in black.

Shirtdress: Button-front styles; unbuttoned for a V neckline, worn at knee length. Side slits and a rounded hem lengthen the line.

T-shirt: Simple and chic in matte jersey; knits with body and drape like midweight cotton interlock or pique. Look for styles with three-quarter-length sleeves.

Drop waist or torso: Skims the line of your body to your hips where the skirt is attached. This construction provides the ease of a straight tunic over your middle and the interest of a flat pleated or softly flared bottom over your hips; knee length keeps it current.

type

F looks

3 show me your closet

Before you begin to rethink your wardrobe, start by having a look at what you already own. More important, before we contemplate any purchases let's assess what to keep and what to toss in order to craft a versatile wardrobe. Every stitch in your closet should ultimately be flattering for your body type and suit your lifestyle.

Reevaluate your wardrobe, one piece at a time. This is the only way to avoid making the same mistakes time and again and to break free of styles that have become habit rather than style enhancing. Most of us have closets stuffed with more than we need or get around to wearing. It's all too easy to get caught up in the illusion (and comfort) that in a stuffed closet we have a wardrobe that is brimming with possibility. In reality, *mess is stress*. An overstuffed closet is chaos as you try to dress. We always want more clothes because the lure of something new, *the next transformation*, is so addictive.

I advocate owning fewer things of better quality. I believe in discernment, especially as we choose the well-cut pieces that are the style bedrock of any well-conceived wardrobe. Our objective is a wardrobe that is fluid. A closet filled with pieces that relate to each other. No new piece joins the party unless you can create *at least* two additional new looks with it. Ideally, there should be a now-and-later quality built in to your choices with fabrics that bridge seasons and time zones.

Think of cleaning your closet as an act of liberation. There are few things more irritating and time consuming than enslavement to a messy closet and drawers. A girl needs a system. She needs to know what the hell is in her closet. A closet sweep is one-half organization and one-half archeology of your self-image.

pruning

I warn you in advance, my approach is hardcore. It's a draconian method that has evolved through trial-and-error editing and organizing of my own clothes as well as years of organizing clothes and accessories for shoots, *and* a large prop closet filled with plastic tubs of the shoes, lingerie, and all kinds of accessories that I use on my jobs. Lest you think I possess the smug satisfaction of a girl whose closets and drawers have always reflected a *Martha-like* organization, I can assure you this is not the case. My closet was once described as the *seventh circle of hell* and my drawers were even more terrifying. I had a chair in my bachelorette bedroom that my husband dubbed "Fresh Kills" (for New York City's massive dumping ground) where I threw my clothes. No more.

My system for a closet sweep

First, if you hang every stitch of clothing you own in your closet at one time (seasons mixed together), begin by grouping everything into categories *by season.*

Within each season then group *by item* (pants, shirts, jackets, dresses, etc.) then finally *by color.* This is an essential system to set up and maintain and the very best way to regularly take stock of what you wear the most and what's getting worn out. Take things out of your closet a season at a time (if you have the seasons other than the

current one stored, wait for the appropriate time to attack them), pile them on the bed, and then, one piece at a time, take a long, hard look.

This may require trying things on, standing in front of a full-length mirror and running through your fit checklist from chapter 1. Let's start with pants. Any pair that hasn't seen daylight in several months needs to be assessed. Be realistic. Ask yourself why you don't wear them. Have they simply been buried, or is it an issue of fit, or a fabric that hasn't worn well? Do they look dated? If you don't love them, leave them.

Let's start four piles

Charity pile: Dated styles, wrong sizes in good condition.

Tailoring pile: Keepers that need a little maintenance, like torn linings, stress at the base of a zipper, hanging hems or cuffs, or any open seams.

Dry cleaning and to-be-stored pile: Anything you don't need right now in this season. Take stock and make a list of what bags and boxes you'll need for storage. Clean everything first. Moths love dirty clothes.

Trash pile: Anything too embarrassing to share with the world at large, like underwear and socks with holes; bras that are stretched or sprung; anything (at the risk of sounding indelicate) that has been indelibly stained; chlorine- or salt-bleached bathing suits; half pairs of cheap hoop earrings; broken pukka shells from seventh grade . . . you get it.

Toss it if

It is the wrong silhouette or proportion: We're not talking about a matter of simple alterations, but rather anything that does not fit in a flattering way because it is wrong for your body type; the construction works against you; an outdated silhouette; something too small, too oversized; any piece that falls into one of your **to avoid** shapes as outlined in chapter 2.

It's road weary: It's been a favorite piece but the fabric is shot. Frequent dry cleaning, for example, has worn the fibers down to a shiny surface along the seams or seat, the fibers are badly pilled from wear across the breasts, seat, between the legs. Take it out of rotation and throw it on the appropriate pile.

> **TIP:** If it has been the pant or skirt fit of your dreams (particularly if good fit is tough for you to find) we'll consider having a tailor use it for a pattern (more on this in chapter 5)

It's a clone: We all do it. Each of us has pieces we buy habitually in the illusive quest for perfect fit. Most closets are choked with dozens of *almost, but not quite right* basics. This is how it is possible for most of us girls to accumulate dozens of black pants (for starters) or to stockpile the same so-so sweater shape (in multiple colors, probably purchased in a flush of excitement at a designer outlet). How about that cluster of overly dry-cleaned white cotton shirts and worn white T-shirts that cross the shade spectrum from faintly yellowed to tinged with gray? Ladies, some weeding!

Pare down those clones, in every category, to retain only those pieces with *truly good fit right now*, in the best quality fabrics, in the best condition:

▶ Flattering and current shapes that give you *variety* in each category including a few daytime options in black and another, also in black, that will take you from work to a night out, for example.

▶ Basic tops and lightweight sweaters edited by color for the best quality and condition, choosing pieces that give you a few different necklines and sleeve lengths in each.

▶ Textured, bulky sweaters should be assessed for the *volume* they add to your body. Do you gain five pounds whenever you put it on? Is it unflatteringly baggy, bulky, or too oversized for your frame? Does it grow baggy on your body as you wear it? If the shape doesn't skim your body, or fall at a flattering place on your hips, *toss it on a pile.*

Any business-appropriate clothing that you edit from your wardrobe can make a difference for women in need. Organizations like Dress for Success Worldwide (**www.dressforsuccess.org**), The Women's Alliance (**www.thewomensalliance.org**) and **www.bottomlessclosetnyc.org** accept businesswear and related accessories (clean and in good condition). It all adds to the network of closets they maintain to help women on welfare prepare appropriate outfits for job interviews. Consider other charitable organizations like the Salvation Army for the rest. And yes, trust a freelancer who lives and dies by receipts to remind you to ask for one when you make a donation, and to file them away for tax time.

▶ Dresses of good quality, with very good fit. Skimming and current or so classic, that they are immune to trends—like your favorite black sheath or a wrap dress, for example.

Tailored jackets and coats require focus and a checklist of their own.

▶ Does it fit well through the shoulders, torso, and arms?
▶ Does it fall at a flattering place on your hips or on your leg?
▶ Does it fit well *and* match or relate tonally to some of your pants and skirts?
▶ Is the fabric stiff or is it supple—does it move with your body when you wear it?

The goal is a focused and versatile selection that you can get at easily every time you dress. Be merciless now—weed out the rest and *add them to your charity pile:*

The color is wrong. People ask if you are feeling well every time you wear it.

A print or pattern does not flatter. Pieces should enhance the body parts they cover.

It looks good, feels bad. As the late, great comic Gilda Radner once said: "I base my fashion taste on what doesn't itch." If you tug and pull or you're hobbled and homicidal, cast it off unless a skilled tailor or cobbler can remedy the source of your misery.

The moment has passed. You've outgrown the look, it's too young for you, not sophisticated enough for the you that you are now. Good-bye, minikilt! Adios Hello Kitty T-shirt.

It gives you an identity crisis. You feel like you're wearing someone else's clothes; a new-you image that you tried on because it was a *must-have* you loved in a fashion editorial. Maybe you were talked into it by an overzealous salesperson. If it doesn't feel like you and it's clear that it never will, don't wear it. Throw it on the charity pile. When you feel inauthentic in something it shows. If it is expensive, a collectible "It" piece, or otherwise *très cher*, sell it on eBay or at a resale shop that specializes in designer labels and recoup some of your cash. For your stylist, it was an expensive sixties vintage Pucci blouse I talked myself into at a Palm Beach shop I visited while on a shoot. When la Pucci joined the other players in my closet her tropical vivacity stood out like the drunk girl at a cocktail party. Hello, eBay.

It's not your size right now. If your weight fluctuates significantly, coming to terms with how many sizes you hang on to at one time is the hardest part of a closet sweep. Again, always, and forever, my philosophy is to appreciate yourself right now and dress yourself well for right now. Hanging on to a range of sizes, small and large, in anticipation of where your body might be a month or six months from now forces you to live in an unsettled, suspended state. Don't do it to yourself. Narrow your things down. Hang on to a size up in a few pairs of very well-cut dark pants and some dark, skimming jeans to **smooth over your psyche during slight weight shifts or PMS.**

Hang on to

The classics: Anything that is immune to trends: a well-cut classic that fits well, is well made, and is in good condition, such as a classic camel-hair coat or a trench coat, a black cashmere sweater, or a simple sheath dress. Any expensive shoe in good condition with a toe and heel that doesn't date like Manolo Blahnik's kitten heel or his pumps with their sinewy, sculpted 2½ to 3⅓ inch heel. *Blahnik's classic designs never change* and are consequently the most widely imitated styles in every price range in the pantheon of shoe design. Approximate the look and keep it in your closet. Take care of your classics, as these are the pieces that add ballast to inexpensive, trendy pieces, and gravity to an eclectic closet. Hang on to classic shapes in prints and patterns that have timeless potential, such as a great leopard print, black-and-white polka dots, black-and-white houndstooth, "status" prints like Pucci, any riff on an Hermès scarf, and, of course, vintage fabrics. These are the things that move in and out of rotation in a wardrobe, at the ready when they are in fashion yet again.

Any designer "It" piece or accessory: The fashion pendulum swings faster each season, meaning that the shelf life of trendy things is short

Trendproof Items

▶ **Classic wool coats**

▶ **Trench coats**

▶ **A classic coat, handbag, or shoes in leopard**

▶ **Cleancut leather jackets and leather car coats**

▶ **Black cashmere turtlenecks, jewel necks**

▶ **Knee-length pencil skirts, A-line skirts**

▶ **A black "tuxedo":** Le Smoking, as the original YSL evening pantsuit was named. Most enduring: a suit with a one-button jacket with medium-width lapels and a just-below-the-bottom length, with a skimming straight pant with the signature tux stripe on each leg.

▶ **Crisp button-front shirts:** In white, menswear stripes, Liberty prints, anything with French cuffs

▶ **Black sheath dresses, wrap dresses**

▶ **Black pumps:** With a classic pointed toe and a sleek 2½ to 3½ inch heel

▶ **Black slingbacks:** with a classic pointed toe, sleek 2½ to 3½ inch heel

▶ **Kitten heels**

▶ **Ballet flats**

▶ **Low-heeled mules**

▶ **Flat, simple thong sandals**

▶ **Hermès and other status silk scarves**

▶ **Classic handbags** (much more on these in chapter 7)

▶ **Levi's 501 Jeans**

but the time it takes for things to recycle is shorter. If something has great lines, great fabric, and most important *makes you look and feel great* whenever you wear it, hang on to it. Pack it away lovingly and wait. **Any vintage designer piece:** If you're savvy enough to be in possession of any mint condition vintage designer pieces that fit, I don't need to tell you to hang on to them—forever.

High style recycling: Good quality and great lines can morph beautifully into something else with the help of a skilled tailor (*see* chapter 5). A dress can be reshaped or transformed into a top, a jacket to a vest, a coat to a belted jacket. You get the picture. When you invest in good design and fabric you can tweak and recycle things into one-of-a-kind takes on a current idea.

Time capsule: I'll cop to my Brownie uniform and a T-shirt collection from every good, bad, and wretched band I've ever seen in concert. It gets worse. There are certain things a girl should never be asked to part with since they are a part of her history. There is always a space somewhere (within reason) for sentiment.

> **TIP:** If you are prone to distraction with every category you unearth or tend to throw yourself sobbing on top of your castoff piles, enlist the help of a good friend. Her objectivity should help keep you pruning.

how to organize your keepers

We return to your closet after you have hung up your keepers by season (if your storage is limited), by item, and last by color . . . here's how I organize my clothing and accessories. This system may work for you too.

In season and in the closet

Uniform hangers: Group your hangers by category as well. Shaped wooden hangers for jackets and coats to maintain the shape of shoulder lines; one kind of heavy plastic hanger for shirts; plastic suit hangers for pants and skirts; soft, padded hangers for silk blouses and dresses you choose to hang. *Not a wire hanger in sight.*

Boxes: Jersey knit dresses, bias cuts, long delicate dresses, vintage pieces, tops with beading. These are things that stretch and lose their shape on the hanger, dust the closet floor, and in general fall apart unless they are folded and boxed. For these, I pack them in tissue in gorgeous boxes I recycle from stores like Thomas Pink, label them on the outer corner of the box, and stack them on my closet shelf (or in storage if out of season).

Sweaters: Folded and stacked by color in stainless-steel wire baskets on my closet shelf. Tissue-weight knits that are easily damaged are stored in individual sweater bags.

Underpants, socks, and tights: Sectioned in drawer dividers that look like a plastic honeycomb. No folding required. Just roll and stuff. Sheer stockings worn and washed are grouped in freezer-sized Ziploc bags.

Bras, silky things, and foundations: Folded in their own drawer. I line it with lavender-scented drawer paper.

Accessories

Shoes/boots: Shoes in heavy rotation in a season hang in a canvas shoe file at the very end of the closet next to my pants (no floor space squandered). Other shoes are kept in their original boxes with a polaroid of the shoe attached to the outer corner and stacked on the closet floor under my shirts. This shoe cataloguing system is a leftover from my magazine fashion closet days and is a cheap solution. I also recommend that you invest in some clear plastic or canvas boxes that you can organize and stack. Next to the shoes, tall boots are grouped together with plastic boot shapers to keep their shape, then shorter boots. I line them up on one of those cedar shoe racks that fit nicely on the floor. Stinky sneakers are dumped in a small canvas storage cube on the closet floor with one of those large mesh sachets filled with volcanic rock that absorbs any trace of their *fragrance.*

Handbags: All bags are stored in felts in a separate cupboard and grouped by size.

- Soft, large leathers are stuffed with old T-shirts to retain their shape.
- Clutches are filed side-by-side like record albums.
- Small evening bags, delicate beaded or embroidered bags are boxed with a layer of tissue paper between them and the box labeled by content

Belts, sunglasses: In their cases (or in Ziploc sandwich bags for cheap street glasses).

Silk scarves and shawls, soft cold-weather hats, other scarves and gloves: Each group has its own plastic box lined with lavender drawer paper and gets labeled. Things stay dust-free, scratch-free, folded, rolled, organized, and easy to lay my hands on. Personally, I find those closet door grids and wall-mounted things an exercise in frustration and inevitable clutter. They have a way of turning into a messy sort of art installation gone bad, and things get too dusty.

Jewelry: Every girl I know has her own collection of *storage vessels* for her jewelry. For me it's straw boxes and jewelry rolls. However you decide to do this, create a way to centralize everything so you're less likely to misplace or lose something you love. If you own a jewelry box, clean it out ruthlessly and organize only what you wear most and what's relevant now.

Anything valuable and delicate remains in its original jewelry box or pouch and squirreled away safely. Another suggestion for storing good jewelry at home—especially when you're away from home (versus a safe deposit at the bank)—is what's known as the *can safe*. These are individual canisters masquerading as cans of everyday household products and are meant to deceive a clueless thief. Your fake can of Comet should not, obviously, be hidden in your lingerie drawer.

Store **the keepsakes and sentimental things** carefully somewhere else. I keep mine in satin pouches from Pearl River Mart, in NYC's Chinatown, and I store them in a series of woven boxes stacked in a part of a bookcase in my bedroom. I keep all my earrings in pairs (!) in a large jewelry roll that has individual pockets. Along with these I store link bracelets and necklaces and small bead necklaces—each in its own pocket. Larger pieces—big beads, costume pearls, big cuff bracelets, bangles—are stored in satin pouches, old shoe felts and Ziplocs in a pinch—each group in its own box.

storage

Note: *Before storing anything, have it cleaned. Moths taught me this the hard way.*

Garment bags: For any clothes you store out of season, hang them on appropriate hangers, dry cleaned, and in garment bags that breathe (either canvas or mesh). Bags treated with moth-repelling lavender or lined with hanging cedar blocks won't leave the grandmotherly scent of mothballs on your clothing.

Space bags: Many clean sweaters to be stored for the season can be packed in one of these babies, the air sucked out of the bag with the vacuum cleaner hose; a footlocker's worth of storage is reduced to the size of a pizza delivery.

Plastic footlockers: Inexpensive and lightweight, they keep things clean and airtight. I use them for bulky winter things. Endlessly useful, providing you have the space for them.

Underbed boxes: Offer less storage but are less space consuming.

clothing care— a few ideas and tips

Buy a clothing steamer (the saving grace of stylists everywhere) and keep it set up (space permitting). Tight on space? Try a handheld travel steamer. Have one at hand and ready to go (minus the water) in or near your closet. Most of us over dry clean and otherwise beat the life out of our clothes as a way to keep them pressed. Creases in knits, silks, woven fabrics, and synthetics steam out in seconds. I even use this method to remove creases in leather and suede. Wrap a piece of cloth (a piece of an old T-shirt works nicely) with a rubber band over the steamer nozzle and apply the steam from the inside against the lining. Apply this same method for velvets, jersey. *Never* iron velvet or jersey knits.

Don't dry clean your white shirts. It yellows the cotton too quickly. I do a white load as needed with only my white cotton shirts and new(ish) white T-shirts. I use OxiClean with my detergent. *(Yes, the very product sold on television by that vaguely frightening and forceful spokesman. It works.)* I take my hanger-dried white shirts to the dry cleaner for pressing only. They stay very white and in good condition far longer.

In my closet I stow a **small plastic toolbox** from the hardware store which contains

- Needles and thread, along with a pair of small nipper scissors to trim any threads.
- A Ziploc full of all of those thread/button combos that were attached to sweaters, jackets, shirts, coats, and so on, when I bought them. I staple them to the price tag and write a quick description of what it belongs with as I know I will never remember.
- A shoe buffing cloth and brush, shoe polish in black and brown, and a bottle of Mr. Leather to clean shoes and bags. All shoes get a quick going over before every wearing.
- A Helmac lint roller at the ready (I have pugs; they shed like buffalos).

A mesh bag for laundering the "fine washables" I am entirely too lazy to do by hand. Look for a bag that has a built-in floating disk that keeps the bag buoyant at the top of the washload so everything within is cleaned gently. This goes in a gentle cold water cycle with Delicare or Woolite once a week and onto a drying rack in the tub.

A mesh sweater dryer to hand-wash and block sweaters. I found one that folds up into a small circle and springs open to a large surface when needed.

My preferred shopping method for these organizational tools? As few stops as necessary. Here are some Web sites that can help you assemble what you'll need to get the job done.

- **goodmans.net:** For steamers—look for the Jiffy JF J200 with a plastic head and bottle. Conair makes a good one—the GS10. Portable steamers are hit or miss. The Jiffy JF 0601 portable E-Steam is, in my experience, the very best travel steamer and I've used 'em all! Never travel without it.
- **hometrendscatalog.com:** Everything I've mentioned and then some.
- **containerstore.com**
- **bedbathandbeyond.com**
- **target.com**
- **potterybarn.com**
- **crateandbarrel.com**

- **lillianvernon.com:** Jewelry rolls, hanging jewelry bags, (garden gnomes).
- **pearlriver.com:** Satin jewelry bags, jewelry rolls.
- **buyasafe.com:** Can safes (usually about twenty dollars).
- **labouquetiere.com:** Scented drawer papers, luxe laundry items, and a lot of other girly indulgences for a well-deserved reward for all this hard work.

As banal as all this stuff may seem, it's important and timesaving to set up a system that works for you every day—keep up with it, sort things carefully and seasonally *so that you never have to go through this again!* Then, the trick, I believe, is to tweak things incrementally. When you add a few new pieces, edit out a few old pieces. Know what you own and wear all of what you own and the whole concept of a wardrobe (rather than a closet crammed with stuff) becomes satisfying and enhancing rather than a source of stress. ●

4 how to shop like a stylist

Choosing what to wear involves more than just covering our bodies or presenting the appropriate image of ourselves to the world—it is loaded with emotion. We all want our clothes to make us look gorgeous, shapely, and confident. Chances are, if you're reading this book, you are aware that the clothes you wear have the power to convey a great deal about your personality, your outlook, and your self-image.

The editorial and advertising images that catch our eye are often more about transmitting fantasy images—an idealized vision of fashion and style—than they are about the clothes and accessories themselves. And that's where most of us get tripped up. Who hasn't been seduced into buying something that didn't truly fit or flatter her body all for the sake of hopping on a trend or trying to capture a fantasy torn from the pages of a magazine? Advertisers spend billions annually to ensure that this happens whenever we flip through fashion pages. Buying into an image that's not authentically you is a certain way to fill your closet with things you won't wear more than a few times. As aware as American women have become about designer labels, we've all been suckered at one time or another by big-time marketing.

In this chapter, I'll help you avoid the pitfalls of shopping as an amateur in what has become a professional's game. I'll apply the same strategy shopping with you that I do when shopping for my private clients: women in television, film actresses, and business executives. For you and for them the goal is the same: to find pieces that create a fluid balance between well-cut, current, day-to-day style and carefully edited trends that will work with your body shape and your reality. To best assemble this mix, my eye is trained on the small details as well as the broad strokes, on the distinctions between what's well made—in all price ranges—and what's not.

Seemingly "effortless" style is a fantasy, an imagined state of fashion euphoria where every stitch of your wardrobe magically coordinates. It's always somehow described in fashion magazines as easily accessible for any woman. It's not. Effortless style requires some effort. Listen, I love a recreational stroll through the stores as much as the next girl, letting my eyes roam over what looks appealing. What will keep you sane—and help you avoid that glazed over sensation of having seen everything and yet nothing at all—is to *shop with a plan*. In every season, on any shopping trip, *think first about the shapes and proportions that are best for your body.* Then give some savvy regard to how the trends can translate into new looks that boost your ego and suit every aspect of your life. We will create the foundation for a wardrobe that will take you to work or play.

Your plan begins with making a list of the things you really need—maybe updating some of the beloved shopworn pieces you've cleared from your closet—along with anything in the magazines that you think you must have. Ask yourself a few questions that I'd ask you if you were my client (and you are): What do your clothes need to do for you? What image do you want to project? Not just at work but in all aspects of your life. What do you want to accentuate about your body and what do you want to smooth out, skim over, or downplay?

Let's take stock of your focal points from top to bottom. Always think about your tops as a frame for your face, neck, and décolletage. Choose only those colors that boost your skin tone. If you've got a great bust line, for example, hone in not only on necklines that accentuate your shoulders and a bit of décolletage, but look for pieces with curvy constructions cut on the diagonal to compliment your feminine shape. Think Bardot rather than *Baywatch*. If your waist is defined, accentuate it with a belt or sash and look for constructions with a nipped waist or that are tapered. If your legs are good, raise that hemline a tick. Always choose **your** best length—your comfort level—regardless of what's just come down the runway.

WITH YOUR WISH LIST, *The Pocket Stylist,* and those focal points in mind, let's take a virtual walk through a department store. Even if the designer floor is out of reach financially or the sizing is wrong, we'll still look first at what is happening in the expensive collections. Don't worry for one second about aggressive salespeople bugging you.

Simply tell them that you don't need their help, thank you (unless you do, of course), that you are looking for ideas. Period. *This is research.*

When I style shoots for advertising clients, for example, I'm given a wish list of looks (and about twenty pages pulled from fashion magazines) that outline the desired look for the model's wardrobe. This is obviously a critical part of the overall image the ad is meant to project. Often the requested look is something "very Calvin" but I've been given a Kmart budget. I'm asked to produce looks that approximate the real thing. I get the job done by knowing *exactly* what that real thing looks like: the shapes, proportions, and colors so that I can choose the best of the interpretations. I know my *references* and if you're going for a more expensive or designer look for your wardrobe for less (and frankly, who isn't?), you should too.

I'll ask you to make mental notes about the following elements as you peruse the various collections.

- Silhouettes and proportions as they relate to you: focus on the pieces that fall into your list of shapes
- Range of hem lengths
- Fabrics, colors, and textures
- *Dressmaker* or *couture* details: hand stitching, trims, embellishments like embroidery or beading, buttons, hardware, piping along seams, the width of lapels and cuff treatments
- The scale of any prints, the use of novelty fabrics and knits

Take in the sensibility. And we're not just paying attention to the **big looks,** the paradigms of a particular trend that have been featured in every magazine by the time you inspect the real thing on the selling floor. Rather, we'll closely inspect the cuts of the foundation pieces (or commercial pieces as they are known in the biz): tailored jackets, well-cut skirts and pants, luxe sweaters, and soft blouses are the **indispensable pieces** that give breadth to the collection as a whole and provide a subtle way to mix solid tailoring with runway whimsy.

Designers are always thinking about the most comprehensive presentation of their clothes. After all, the more options they provide us with, the more combinations we may buy. We'll borrow a few of their ideas about proportion, color, and combinations of clean tailoring paired with trends, for example, as a template for the looks we put together more affordably. Observation at the top is always the best way to train your eye to spot the subtle details at more affordable prices.

Stylists and fashion editors are students of fashion. We study clothes. We assess them. I form my impressions by watching clothes on the runway (how they look in motion on the body as much as taking in all the details) and by visiting designers' showrooms where I can look at and touch individual pieces. Take the same opportunity on the selling floor to do your own reconnaissance and to better recognize what really good tailoring and fabric looks like and how it drapes—even on the hanger—particularly if you've never paid close attention to these details before.

Since the trickle-down effect in fashion is now almost immediate, design companies on all rungs of the fashion ladder are poised to spin out more interpretations and line-for-line copies than ever. Here are some things I noted on a recent shopping day: a brocade skirt at Prada had *informed* an affordable lookalike skirt at Theory; Stella McCartney's nude pink jacket with Saville Row pickstitching at the lapel had *inspired* a handy approximation of the same jacket—color, hand stitching, and all—at Equipment; a tuxedo stripe on a pair of Marc Jacobs trousers had inspired the team at Ann Taylor with a subtle piping along the side seams of a pencil skirt; cargo pants at Dior had incited a riot of interpretations everywhere. And so the fashion beat goes on.

Although the runway-to-reality charts in most of the magazines offer capsule comparisons of the runway gear versus lower-priced approximations, there is absolutely no substitute for doing your own detective work, with only *your* body and *your* best shapes and proportions in mind, up close and hands on.

Remember, we're after *your* individual style. Train your eye to recognize the references that will give your clothes a sense of the here and now, with subtle details that are distinctive enough to look special, but not so memorable that you can't wear them *frequently*. Paying attention at the beginning of any season to the details, the references that you can adapt to your wardrobe, means you are better equipped to find expensive-looking, individual pieces in your price range and size range. It also means that you have a focused plan. Don't worry about every trend the style watchers are nattering on about. Take charge of your fit, adapt only what seems relevant, focus on the ideas that will suit your silhouette, and you'll make informed, intelligent decisions.

the indispensables

So, let's start building that look. I always start my search with the *indispensables*, the well-tailored staples: pants, skirts, tops, jackets, clean-cut coats, a dress or two, and jeans. Finding the right foundation pieces often gets overlooked in the hunt for what's trendy at the moment, but they are critical to any well-conceived wardrobe. Until a few of each of these are updated and in place, I don't worry about anything else. You have to bake a cake before you frost it. These are not just generic basics we're after. As the foundation of most of your outfits these pieces should have current cuts and subtle details so that they mix easily with trendy and classic pieces alike. Choose the best fabrics you can afford, to withstand the heavy rotation in your closet and numerous trips to the cleaners.

PANTS: For most of us, great fit in pants is especially hard to pin down. Industry statistics indicate that one in three women is bigger on the bottom than on the top, so it makes sense to spend time finding the right length rise and the right leg cut for the shape of your legs. If you are on a very tight budget you really can get away with just two pairs to start. For day, invest in a sleek, skimming cut in a firm fabric like a lightweight bi-stretch wool gabardine in black or very dark navy. Choose another, slightly fuller-cut trouser in a fabric that drapes like a superfine wool or a wool-and-rayon mix, also in black, to give you both day and evening versatility. Add a range of neutrals like camel, mid- to dark gray, deep wine tones, rich browns, or winter and summer whites, subtle tweeds, or a chalk stripe as you can. If you can swing it, always buy a good cut in a few colors.

Finding the designer(s) and line(s) that cut *your pants* is like money in the bank. Personally, I'd rather buy one great pair of expensive, black *indispensable* pants, wear them into the pavement and have less in my closet, than pull and tug at a closet full of marginal fits and so-so fabrics. *Streamline and buy the best quality you can afford.* Bottom line: if your pants don't fit well, the eye is immediately drawn to the inevitable lines, lumps, and creases. In essence, you're not well dressed. With a few pairs in place, let's move on.

SKIRTS: Have three. Pencil, straight, and A-line are perennials for daytime in a firm, good quality fabric like superfine or a lightweight stretch wool blend. Have one in black and one in another neutral (which can include a subtle chalk stripe or tweed). A bias cut, A-line, or a circle skirt in a fabric with soft drape like matte jersey or silk will take you from the office to an evening out with a quick switch of accessories.

> **TIP:** Always choose the very best length for your leg, whether just above or just below your knee, or longer and falling just above your ankle. Again, it doesn't matter what length just walked down the runway: if it doesn't flatter your leg, leave it alone. Strict midcalf lengths (which surface every so often on the runway) are universally deadly, not to mention a bit frumpy, unless you are built like a runway model.

MIXABLE TOPS: Along with the essential crisp white shirt and white and black T-shirts, add a few good quality solid knits in the necklines that suit you best. Choose lightweights like merino or cashmere for a versatile and seasonless quality. Have one in black. Choose another in a skin-flattering neutral, and one in a clear, rich color that boosts your skin tone and sparks those neutral bottoms. Choose at least one knit with a round or low oval neckline to layer over the white shirt for the forever chic collar-and-cuffs look. All three should be lightweight enough for no-bulk layers under a shirt and jacket.

This is where you can always save. Paying designer prices for simple, flat knits, cotton T-shirts, or white cotton shirts (even if you have it to spend) is consumer insanity. (Let's put your money into a more visible piece like a good jacket, for example.) You can always find current-looking, well-made tops at Club Monaco or Banana Republic for starters, where the quality is good, the price is right, and the basics often have a little something extra: a subtle pleating at the base of turtleneck, a wide sleeve or a gathered wrist on a long sleeve T-shirt. These are just the kind of subtle designer treatments that mix well with anything, expensive or otherwise. Needless to say, check J. Crew, Mexx, and the Gap while you're out with your credit cards.

JACKETS: When everything else in your closet turns on you, nothing pulls together, anchors, or creates an outfit faster than a beautifully cut jacket. Invest as much as you can in good fabric and tailoring for at least one jacket that raises the bar in your closet. Be very choosy about proportion and fit since few things torpedo a look faster than a jacket that looks cheap or that fits poorly. Ideally, your finest jacket should match a daytime pant or skirt (as in suit) depending upon your dress code at work.

For most corporate women, the concept of *suit* has evolved into combinations of separates rather than a wardrobe of matched jackets and bottoms. The silhouettes are now much easier. Many jackets, in refined fabrics, are styled with a blouselike quality or borrow from casual sport shapes like bombers, windbreakers, or zip-front vests. Feminine skirt shapes like circle, pencil, draped A-lines, bias, and soft pleats balance tailored jackets. Sweaters often replace jackets altogether.

If you work in an ultraconservative environment with a narrowly defined dress code, respect the culture, of course, but by all means wear suits in very current shapes. Assert a sense of appropriate but individual style to distinguish yourself from a look of bland conformity. Push the boundaries in favor of fashion and skip the conventional and boxy menswear-for-women cuts. I'm always astonished that I still see bad eighties throwbacks like this on the racks, but they are there. Always have your suits tailored to perfection. (We'll talk about accessories in chapter 7.)

TIP. A well cut pantsuit (that fits to the teeth) in a seasonless-weight wool in either black, white, or ivory means never begging off an evening invitation because you had **nothing to wear.** Other good fabric options: wool and silk blends, cotton sateen.

COATS: Think amortization. Invest as much as you possibly can in quality and tailoring and then congratulate yourself for your thrift when the cost per wear goes down after a few years and it still looks great. Whether you walk dozens of city blocks to work or from your car through a parking lot, your coat makes an indelible first and last impression. It hardly matters how well dressed you may be underneath: an ill-fitting coat sabotages your whole look.

A girl can finesse anything in a sharp coat, like the legendary Broadway actress who once requested that her purchases from a posh Fifth Avenue store be delivered for a lunchtime fitting at a theater

How to Fit a Jacket

Over years of styling sittings for magazines, catalogues (sometimes romancing inexpensive clothes), and ad shoots (with budgets that demand trial-and-error shopping for commercials), I've learned some valuable things about fit. Watching the fitting process in Seventh Avenue design studios was an early education. Here's something I learned from a friend who has designed for big sellers Ann Taylor, Liz Claiborne, and Finity to name a few. When you try on a jacket or a coat it should feel *plumb*. What does plumb feel like? Think of any piece you've owned or tried on that seemed to slide over your body, the collar molded to your neck, the shoulder line precisely cut to meet the edge of your shoulders: you felt a delicious drape on your body. Plumb means an ideal vertical line against your body so that the hem of a garment hangs evenly. (If it hikes in the front it will hang long in the back, if it hikes in the back it will hang long in the front—either way, put it back.)

First, check the shoulder line. Great fit here is the linchpin of any fitted jacket's overall proportion on your body. The shoulder line of any jacket style should meet the edge of your shoulders. For the most accurate gauge of overall fit remember to wear a top of the same weight you'll most frequently layer underneath. Look for tailoring features: a nipped waist, vertical seams, or panels that install shape for a skimming fit. A drop shoulder jacket is a somewhat trickier fit to define. Although the shoulder line has been designed to hang below the edge of your shoulders, the seams should fall no more than 1 to 2 inches below your shoulder bones to avoid looking dumpy. It's important to take the cut and the overall proportion into consideration and choose a fit that still skims and defines your body.

Does it have reach and lift? Can you raise your arms (as if to sling a bag over your shoulder or grab for something) without tightness through the shoulders and back? No? Try the next size. If a jacket pitches forward or rolls back on your shoulders as you move, put it back on the rack. Most likely it was fit on a body with a broader shoulder line or the length from the shoulder to the underarm is too long for you and consequently the fit will never be right.

Check the stance: Stance is a tailoring term for the meeting point of the lapel and buttons. How long is the V line? Most girls of average height or taller—at any size—look great in a one- or two-button jacket for the longer line it creates; a deep V that draws the eye up and down and flatters a full bustline. Shorter girls and petites appear taller in a higher

principles of plumb

collar molds to your neck

fit starts here: shoulder line

a flattering stance

is the length flattering?

stance—at midchest—with small- to medium-width lapels and with three- or even four-button styles.

Length: Universally flattering jacket lengths include cropped at or just below the waist, at the high hip to hipbone, at an inch below your bottom, and at fingertip length, meaning where your fingertips rest on your thigh when you stand with your arms relaxed and straight at your side. Most of us have a low hip span—our widest point where our hips and bottom meet—that visually expands our overall line if the eye is drawn there by a hemline. Any jacket that hits this point on your body should go back on the rack.

district restaurant. When a greenhorn stylist dispatched from the store's fashion office struggled into the restaurant with bulging garment bags she found the actress waiting at the bar in a timeless Burberry trench. The actress directed the stylist to the ladies' room for an expedient fitting. The actress peeled off her coat, revealing that she was quite naked underneath. They quickly got through the fitting and the stylist hoofed the clothes back to the store. The actress put her trench back on and returned to her drink at the bar.

Seasonless Coats: Since we're on the subject, owning any riff on a **trench coat** is the **ultimate indispensable**. A trench finishes your staple looks, is clean enough to mix with your trendiest pieces, and

How to Fit a Coat

When you try on a coat, *wear clothes underneath* for an accurate fit. If it's July and you're in a cotton camisole (depending on how you'll need to layer underneath) grab a sweater or jacket from a neighboring rack. Apply all the principles of plumb which we discussed with jackets, as well as:

▶ **Test your mobility:** Again it's about **reach and lift—** raise your arms and cross them in front of you. If it pulls through the shoulders and back then try the next size. Find a three-way mirror and move around checking the shoulder line and the collar. Do the arms look skimming, graceful? Take in the overall effect. Does the coat drape and move with your body or is it stiff?

▶ **Choose the right proportion:** Does the length work with your longer skirts? If it works with them it will accommodate any width pant leg. Does the silhouette create a flattering unbroken line for your shape?

▶ **Check the sleeve length:** Long enough, for a traditional-length sleeve, means clearing the top of your hand or the top of a glove.

When you buy a parka, a quilted coat, or a shearling the same principles apply. The shoulder line and skimming fit should be the same as above. This will ensure that you don't look like the Michelin man.

versatile enough for day and night. Along with lightweight wool and cotton canvas, a clean, **knee-length coat** in glove leather or a soft suede is an investment piece that goes anywhere and with very clean lines and simple styling, will never date. Choose a good quality skin, however, as bargain leather and suede can look very stiff and the finish can be too plastic or sandpapery.

> **TIP:** Buy a $30 insurance policy—have your skins waterproofed at the dry cleaner before wearing.

Winter coats: Whether you choose wool, cashmere, camel hair, or tweed, any of these tried-and-true classics should have a good hand, meaning the fabric should feel supple and substantial.

> **TIP:** Try my twenty-second test: take a handful of fabric and squeeze hard for a good twenty seconds. Inexpensive wool will look like a crumpled lunch bag (and so will your butt after sitting). My stealth squeezing may not endear me to the sales staff but I never look crumpled and neither do my clients. Especially if you're on a tight budget, your stylist encourages you to squeeze all questionable wool coats or otherwise.

Timing is everything. If you can hold out, wait for the November sales to buy your expensive coat. For shearling, shop in June for a classic at a sharply reduced price. Store it and be ready for the first plunge in temperature.

DRESSES: You need a great dress in your closet if you like the way you look in a dress. But if one-piece dressing presents a proportions challenge for you, then choose separates in the same fabric that create a dress silhouette on your body. Solids or a flattering geometric print can achieve the same unbroken line. The importance of a little black dress (LBD in fashion shorthand) in your closet is no fashion overstatement however. Yours can be one or two pieces, but do have something in your wardrobe that serves as a definitive and chic no-brainer whenever you need a quick solution for an invitation.

JEANS: Both indispensable and trendy, versatility makes jeans the most everpresent mixable piece in most of our closets. When I'm styling a shoot where the model or subject will wear jeans, I pull together at least a dozen pairs to arrive at an ideal fit. Does this sound like your last attempt at finding the right pair?

Girls, please watch out for ultralow, *butt-crack-revealing* low riders. A 6½ or 7 inch (or otherwise insignificant) rise breaks up the body line with an expanse of skin between the hem of a top and the straight line of a waistband across the low hips. Seen from behind, the effect can make even a slim girl look like she's packing a Sunday roast. Derriere décolletage, plumber's crack avec thong, whatever you call it . . . it's just not a good look, unless it's a part of your tour wardrobe, of course.

Most civilians (as we non-models, nonactresses, nonsingers are known)—of all sizes—look pretty damn good in a pair of dark indigo bootcuts or slight flares (for hip balance) hitting at the low waist and long enough to wear with at least a one to 1½ inch heel. The fuller your butt, the higher the waistband of the jean should sit on your backside to visually raise your rear view. Not to mention that it's a far better line when you're dressed for speed in a pair of flats or trainers and you don't have the scaffolding effect of a pair of heels!

Whether you are short or tall, curvy or straight, a longer length that brushes the top of your shoe (brushes the toe with heels) and a skimming cut will create a longer, leaner silhouette. Plus, simple old-school styling mixes best with everything. *All girls should run screaming* from high-waist and pleated jeans and anything with a tapered ankle! This construction flatters no one. No other cut has a

How to Fit Your Jeans

Finding a great jeans fit can bring on a migraine if you don't know what you are looking for. As you've undoubtedly discovered, finding the right size doesn't mean you've found the right fit. Here's what I always double check:

- **Rise:** Where the waistband sits. Medium and lower indicate a low waist that rests at the top of your hipbone for missy sizing and at or just below the navel for full-fashion sizing.

- **Waist:** Look for a contoured waist, which starts higher on your behind for a molding, curvy shape and dips down lower in the front. I've seldom seen a woman fail to look good in these.

- **Cut:** How the jeans hug your butt and thighs. Slim and lean usually translate as TIGHT. Stretch and relaxed are generally user friendly, skimming fits.

- **Inner leg seam:** If it's centered it will offer a more conventional fit; if the seam is moved forward slightly, it's very slim; if it's moved back slightly, it will be bit more relaxed.

- **Leg openings:** The width of the opening at the ankle.

- **Bootcut:** Hip-balancing, straight, full width at the ankle and the flattering friend of most girls at any size.

- **Flares:** Hip balance that is best for medium height to tall girls; and with a bit of ease through the hips and thigh, universally flattering.

- **Drainpipe:** A very tight leg, the same width from top to bottom is a cut worn best by the slimmest girls.

- **Commit to a length:** The jeans that are long enough to wear with high heels should not be the same pair you wear with flats or sneakers and sweeping up the sidewalk. There are two ways you can go for shortening your jeans. Cost-free and efficient, cut them at a desired length for either heels or flats and let them fray naturally. This works for casual wear and casual workplaces. For the finished approach, have them hemmed in the same color stitching at the drycleaner for a cheap and simple solution. Huge cuffs on jeans, unless you are very tall and very thin, always have a leg-shortening and booty-widening effect. I want to cry when I see an otherwise great-looking girl throw off her body line with this style misstep. Hem them, and streamline those legs in your denims.

And now, a quick review:

A Bare Bones Checklist of the Indispensables You Need in Your Wardrobe

Two pairs of dark pants
- Simple, skimming cut in a crisp fabric for day
- Fuller leg in a fabric that drapes in black for day and evening

Two pairs of jeans
- One hemmed to wear with heels
- One hemmed to wear with flats, sneakers

Three skirts
- Clean lines like a pencil, trouser, or an A-line in black or in lightweight wool
- A-line, bias, or circle in a fabric with drape for day and evening
- Neutral in a mixable fabric which can include a subtle chalk stripe or tweed

A white button-front shirt and T-shirts (of course)

Three sweaters (seasonless, lightweight merino or cashmere)
- Black (must tonally match your black bottoms—*see* Colors)
- Another neutral choice—skin-flattering, of course
- Rich color

Two jackets
- Tailored jacket that matches one pair of your dark pants (read: suit, black is always a good bet)
- Sporty shape in a refined fabric, like a bomber, motorcycle jacket, or windbreaker style in leather, suede, corduroy, soft wool, cotton twill—goes to work and works for play

Three coats
- Trench coat or any riff on this classic that flatters you both for rain and between seasons in a light neutral or black
- Between seasons knee-length coat that works day or night; in leather, suede, tropical-weight wool
- Winter coat (a regional consideration, of course) in the very best fabric you can possibly afford

Dress or matching separates that create a dress silhouette. Always have something that serves as a Little Black Dress in your closet.

A Word or Two About Color

All your color choices for clothing (and cosmetics) should be informed by your natural skin tone. More than likely, you've been color printed or received some guidance (hopefully, knowledgeable) at a cosmetics counter to determine if your skin tone is either warm (yellow/orange based) or cool (blue/red based). Not sure? In daylight, look closely at the skin on your face (clean of any makeup) and your entire body. Every skin tone is a combination of red, brown, and yellow pigments. The predominant tone or color just under your skin is what determines if you have blue-pink-red undertones or yellow-orange-brown undertones. Obviously, the colors you choose to wear next to your face and neck should complement your natural tones. Never trust the fluorescent lights in fitting rooms. If something seems flattering, buy it, but always double check it in daylight against your face, neck, and chest (again, clean of any makeup) before your wear it.

When combining pieces in monochromatic or tonal combinations, don't forget to check your color values. Remember, there are warm and cool undertones blended into fabrics as well. Mixing a cool, gray-toned brown with a warm, red-toned brown, for instance, will look pretty dreadful. Mixes of black with black, or white with white—known as achromatics—must have compatible values as well. Mixing a black with dark blue undertones with a black with undertones of dark brown looks just plain dirty. How can you tell? Again, you should always compare monochromatic colors in daylight. Confine any colors that give your face a hepatitis C–like pallor (usual suspects for many of us: beige, olive, taupe) to your bottoms.

more widening and leg-shortening effect. Watch out for very light washes, tricky engineered fading, and whiskering at the crotch (who came up with this one?). The *faux*-aged effect and light patches on your thighs and butt can act like a *high beam* on areas most of us should think twice about spotlighting. Wearing your jeans as a *stand-in* for your sweatpants, too long and bunching over the top of chunky workout sneakers, is another way your body line will look blocky.

FOR CONTINUITY IN YOUR WARDROBE—top to bottom—keep your indispensables updated to reflect the subtle shifts in silhouette that happen every few seasons. They should always be in lockstep with the trendier things—like accessories—that you pair them with. This is how a look really gels. Again, girls, don't skimp here. Invest in **fit**, in good quality fabrics that won't wrinkle or pill, and in shapes that will have a good run in your closet. Spend a lot less on trends that will move in and out of fashion—and your closet—at warp speed.

where to shop for your indispensables

When I'm shopping for any project, I look everywhere and anywhere: department stores, designer boutiques, small boutiques, specialty stores, high-priced and midpriced lines, the discount houses that stock designers' past season merchandise, and closeouts, like Century 21 in New York. But for the indispensable pieces, I often head straight to the modern bridge lines for prices just below designer.

The concept of *bridge* was devised by manufacturers to offer a bridge between the higher prices of designer collections and the next price category known as *better*. In the bridge lines you'll find quality fabrics, many of the same references, and often a more democratic fit. I always comb these collections for individual pieces or *items* (in retail-speak) with sophisticated styling and subtle details that elevate the bargains and mix seamlessly with designer pieces: *exactly the qualities you need in an indispensable piece.*

Since versions of the same seasonal shapes and fabrics found in Donna Karan's and Ralph Lauren's collections (in particular) appear in their bridge lines, I usually hit pay dirt with individual pieces worth investing in: pants and skirts cut like their more expensive collection counterparts in similar fabrics, often with similar details, along with jackets and coats with the same "collection" sensibility for roughly half the price. But keep this in mind: Design companies on every rung of the ladder, at every price level, have their sights trained on whoever sells, meaning when you have an informed eye, you're apt to find things wherever you look. You'll be shopping like a stylist—your own.

Bridge Lines for Body Types A, B, or C:

Akris Punto	Hugo, Hugo Boss
Anne Klein	Kulson
Barney's Private Label	Piazza Sempione
Chaiken	Ralph Lauren Blue Label
DKNY	Strenesse Gabriele Strehle
Elie Tahari	Theory
Farhi, Nicole Farhi	TseSay

Better lines and comparable pricing for Body Types A, B, or C:

The "Better" Market is the part of the retail world poised for a considerable upgrade with the addition of hip and affordable collections by top designers. Watch for new lines from Marc Jacobs, Michael Kors, and Calvin Klein to arrive in stores in 2004. Have a look at these "modern" Better lines/stores for A, B, and C.

Perry Ellis: After a decade out of the picture, new design has revived this label with the kind of chic, modern separates any girl wants in her closet (Spring 2004).

H by Tommy Hilfiger: Clean and sophisticated separates (Spring 2004).

CITY DKNY: Many of the same shapes that appear in DKNY in a season.

AK Anne Klein: Strong on affordable leather pieces, staples in good, subtle fabrics.

Nine West: As their shoes improve, so does their ready-to-wear. Outerwear is especially good.

Kenneth Cole: Clean reliable shapes with a mixture of street, preppy, and Prada references. Fabric and fit is hit or miss.

Hennes Woman/H&M stores: Comb through carefully for current shapes and references. Pieces are built for a look, not necessarily to last.

Mexx: A well-established chain in Europe and Canada enters the U.S. in 2003–04. Trends and clean-lined indispensables alike, for work and otherwise.

Club Monaco: Strong on designer details and direct interpretations of big-ticket items in any season.

Zara: Stick with the Zara Woman line. Along with those right-off-the-runway looks, you cannot beat a Spanish company for affordable and often convincing leather jackets/coats. For tailored pieces, use the 20-second test on wools and look for fabrics with low shine, as many styles have a high synthetic content.

J.Crew: Along with all the casual gear, don't forget the seasonal selection of very well-cut pants, skirts, jackets in fabrics like super-weight wool and gabardine, offered in petites and tall. (Don't overlook the suiting separates and coats offered in the catalogue only.)

Banana Republic: Their strength is well-cut, tailored pieces in good fabrics (the volume they produce gives them access to some of Italy's best fabric mills). Stick with solids; go easy on the "fashion" items, or watch yourself coming and going everywhere.

> **TIP:** Remember, the less the fabric costs, the more pieces produced; then the less reliable the sizing may be and the greater the need for tailoring to clinch the fit.

Online:

Have a look at these resources.

ShopDex.com   eLUXURY.com
StyleShop.com   yoox.com
Bluefly.com   LuxLook.com

Body Types D, E, or F:

It's no news flash for any woman who shops the plus-sized market that the short supply of lines that offer great tailoring and fabrics in current shapes lags far behind demand. Search out specialty stores and small independents who offer made-to-measure options. You'll find a more individualistic approach from smaller designers that the department stores, frankly, don't have the vision or courage to buy.

If you generally shop women's lines, never rule out missy departments and, particularly, department stores' private label collections for tops. I often find sweater tunics in XL, for instance, that fit curvy girls like a sexy, high-hip length top. Missy sized 16 and 18 bottoms and tops with stretch are always worth a look. In fact, girls, I could fill another book on this segment of the retail world but for now here are some recommendations based on my shopping for full-fashioned women who want more than conventional boxy shapes, appliquéd T-shirts, and pull-on pants. Again, my focus for voluptuous girls is to create a gorgeous body line, to choose shapes and fabrics that work with the body and skim the curves. I'll always choose mono-chromatics or tonal combinations layered with subtle textures first, and then add luxe, knockout accessories (*see* chapter 7).

When I shop for curvy girls, I much prefer the selection and experience at specialty stores where there is a focus on quality and fit, rather than size alone. As designer Sylvia Heisel, whose name-sake store in SoHo, in New York City, offers made-to-measure, once explained it to me: "I'm not focused on size. I'm interested in the line my clothes create on a woman's body—at any size—and the way the colors I choose complement her skin tone."

Most critical, there is an eye to buying what looks sophisti-cated at the smaller stores. I've found that the trick to weeding through the full-fashion market as it struggles to further define itself, is to avoid the pieces that are overdesigned with a lot of silly junior market, teen gimmicks. Stick with sophisticated shapes in solids. Opt for subtle textures and choose those prints that closely resemble what is going on in the designer departments. You'll find them when you've familiarized yourself with the seasonal refer-ences. Keep it simple and you can't miss.

Here are the specialty stores and specialty lines I always have a look at.

Marina Rinaldi: Hands down, the best investment resource for current-looking indispensables and takes on the seasonal trends alike.

Anna Scholz: Although sold in department stores in her native Britain and throughout Europe, Anna is a specialty store find here in the United States. It's well worth looking for her modern shapes, cash-meres, luxurious fabrics, and great fit.

Richard Metzger: Artfully designed bias constructions, sophisticated shapes, beautiful fabrics in looks for day and evening.

Gianfranco Ferre Forma: Well-tailored jackets, pants and skirts, leather coats.

Jeans

Suggested Brands for All Body Types

Here are the lines in various price ranges I always look at.

HIGH END

D Squared: Innovative styling, great fit.

Ant: Contoured fit, simple styling, simply cool.

Rogan: Well-cut, deceptively tailored simplicity, the essence of "old school."

paper, denim & cloth: Clean fit, clean styling.

Habitual: Look for the simplest styles, good realistic fit.

Diesel Denim Gallery: Great cuts and finishes.

Citizens of Humanity: Their bootcuts and flares have a very nice, clean fit.

Beau Dawson: Ideal missy fit with a very current shape, groovy styling.

MIDPRICE

Marc by Marc Jacobs: Simple 5 pocket styles, flattering democratic fit.

Diesel: Skip the over-the-top styling; they also have simple things with good fit.

Levi's Premium Quincy Boot Cut Jeans

Levi's Red Tab Boot Cut: Has a contoured waist.

A/X Armani Exchange: Bootcuts.

Polo Jeans Co.: Bootcuts and flares.

Tommy Jeans: Missy and full-fashion bootcuts and flares and not a tapered leg in sight, reliable fit.

GOOD BUYS

H&M: Simple styles for all body types from average to the BIB (Big Is Beautiful) collection.

French Connection: Slim, contemporary fit.

J.Crew: Stretch hip bootcut, stretch hipster flare.

Silver Jeans: Great contoured fit based on waist and inseam measurements.

Banana Republic: Excellent missy fit up to size 16 in most styles.

Victoria's Secret catalogue: "The Curve": a contoured waist, great for all girls up to missy size 16.

Lane Bryant: The best-fitting, best-looking full-fashion jeans out there.

Jalate: Good full-fashion fit, but skip those bells and whistles and the junior market gimmicks.

Paris Blues: Full fashion, pass on the bells and whistles and gimmicks.

Newport News catalogue: Their Jeanology line offers full-fashion slim fit, bootcuts up to 26 W and low-rise flares up to missy 16 and tall missy 18.

Alight.com: A selection of jeans styles from different designers.

Sylvia Heisel: Dresses and coats are a specialty in beautiful fabrics and colors, sold at her namesake store and specialty stores around the country.

H&M: Their Big Is Beautiful line—look through it—changes frequently and includes current indispensables.

Lane Bryant: Jeans, simple pants with clean lines.

At department stores, I always comb through these collections for current-looking indispensable pieces with trend references.

I.N.C.: Offers many of the same pieces found in the I.N.C. missy line in the season, like jackets with seaming for shape, well-cut pants with subtle lace trims, satin bias and circle skirts, and satin coats. Use the twenty-second test on wools.

Emme: Filled with current shapes in great quality fabrics like stretch Ultrasuede, faux leather, shot wools, and jersey. Expensive-looking details like top stitching, ruching, pintucking. Look for the flat-front bi-stretch bootcut pant (this is the best pant of its kind I've seen for curvy girls), and the power cami for a smooth finish under tops.

Company Ellen Tracy: Shop one item at a time, very true woman's cut in denim jeans, mixable, simple sweaters and good outerwear pieces.

Lafayette 148: Current cuts in jackets, pants; great fabrics.

Ellen Tracy: Conservative but a good source for elegant, mixable coats, and very well-cut jackets.

TIP: For tall, curvy girls I always take a look in the men's department. Stay clear of anything oversized and baggy, however. Look for sweaters and shirts that have a tapered cut. They'll give you a skimming look with pants or a pencil skirt and heels. One of the many dirty little secrets of ready-to-wear is that men's collections are less expensive and often better made than women's wear. At the designer level, Helmut Lang, YSL, Gucci, Prada, and Marc Jacobs are all lines to look through for shirts and sweaters in solid, seasonal trend colors. Club Monaco, Zara, H&M, and Express are always worth a look for their interpretations of the expensive labels listed earlier.

Dana Buchman: Good tailoring and trend references alike.

Alfani Woman: Current pant shapes, jackets, toppers.

Tadashi: Good leather pieces and tailored jackets, pencil skirts and well-cut pants.

Anne Klein: Classics and trend references, a good source for mixable, indispensable pieces.

Tommy Hilfiger: Trends and classics alike in outerwear, sweaters, skirts, pants.

Lauren, Ralph Lauren: Outerwear and sweater coats.

Eileen Fisher: Luxe-looking boiled-wool jackets and coats to wear with anything you own.

I have ordered (with good results) from these catalogues and online resources.

Neiman Marcus by Mail

Garnet Hill (private label up to missy 18)

Bloomingdale's by Mail

Newport News: Simple solid tops, sweaters, clean wide leg trousers.

Alight.com: Offerings from different designers, look for dresses from Emme, Alex Evenings, Donna Ricco, and Kathryn Connover.

SizeAppeal.com: Dresses and separates with a contemporary junior fit, so, in general, size up one.

Kiyonna.com: Dresses.

double agents

Any piece that blurs the distinction between the clothes you need for work and what you can use for the rest of your life. A fluid wardrobe is always filled with key pieces that are adaptable for just about any situation.

Eye catchers: Familiar shapes and cuts like a tailored jacket, flared trouser, an A-line skirt, or a knee-length coat in fabrications like brocade, tapestry, printed cottons, colorful printed velvets, embellished wools shot with metallic thread or sequins, fur or faux fur trims. A few distinctive pieces add focal points to a wardrobe and are mixable with pieces high and low.

Sport shapes in refined fabrics: Blousons, bombers, windbreakers, motocross shapes, and zip-front vests in fabrics like glove leather, soft suede with knit banding at the neck or hips, canvas with leather trims, cashmere, wool, fur, faux fur, silks, or satin for a work-and-play versatility and a boost for indispensable skirts and pants.

Strict tailoring in casual, unexpected fabrics: Fitted jackets, pencil skirts, and trouser cuts in indigo and colored denim, lightweight corduroy, sport nylons, print cottons, seersucker, engineer stripes, or rough, textured linens.

Sweaters with jacket styling: Shapes like the bomber, Chanel, motocross, peacoat, and blouson with details like unusual expensive-looking buttons, zippers, snaps; suede or leather trims like slash or patch pockets, panels, epaulettes, and rib knit trims at the neck, waist, or hip.

Reversible: Double-faced jacket and skirt constructions that reverse from solid to tweed, leather to suede, or solid to print for value and versatility.

Finished tops: With dressmaker details like shirring, pleating, ruching, or pintucking that add texture and shape to silk knits, tissue-weight merino wools or cotton button downs; tops cut on the diagonal for a draped, curvy fit; wrap shirts with stretch, blouson styling in silk; any top that can stand in for the bodice of a dress when paired with a skirt, soften the look of a suit or add a feminine charm to a jacket and jeans.

TIP: To minimize a full bust or torso try a button-front style with shirring along the placket or tops that are cut on the diagonal with ruching along a side seam, worn at hipbone length.

When you are focused on double agents, you'll notice that most lines offer some pieces designed to do it all in your closet.

Double Agents for Body Types A, B, or C:

Again, the "modern" bridge and better lines are always a good bet (refer to your indespensibles lists). Have a look at these collections/stores as well, representing prices from designer to better:

Alice + Olivia	**Moschino Cheap N' Chic**
Cacharel	**Paul & Joe**

Catherine Malandrino	Peter Som
Diane von Furstenberg	Proenza Schouler
FAL	Rebecca Taylor
French Connection	Temperley
ICB by Victor & Rolf	Tibi
Marc by Marc Jacobs	Tocca
Mayle	White + Warren
Mint	Y3

Double Agents for Body Types D, E, or F:

Refer to your indispensables list but pay particular attention to:

Anne Scholtz	H&M Stores—BIB Big is Beautiful
Anne Klein Woman	I.N.C.
Bloomingdale's by Mail	Lauren, Ralph Lauren Woman
Company Ellen Tracy Woman	Marina Rinaldi
Dana Buchman	Neiman Marcus by Mail
Emme	Tommy Hilfiger Woman

Garnet Hill Catalog (private label up to missy 18)

As your stylist likes to say, *"look under every rock!"* Again, you can find good individual pieces just about anywhere. No one clothing line can do it all for us—shop a few pieces at a time and build your wardrobe with care.

bargain hunting

▶ **Choose natural fibers:** Democratic fabrics like denim, cotton, corduroy, silks, and wool blends with a matte finish are always less telling than most synthetic fabrics.

▶ **Choose dark colors:** Along with blended colors, cosmetic pastels, and white. Inexpensive primary colors can look very cheap. Club Monaco and Zara are both masters at capturing the look of designer colors in a season.

▶ **Check the seams:** This is always one of the biggest giveaways, as expensive sewing is flat and nearly invisible. Inexpensive seams can look as if they are rolling in or puckered; bunchy. If you have to have it, take it to the cleaners for a professional press. If the problem isn't smoothed out enough to look flat, take it back; it will never look right.

▶ **How's the lining?** Make sure that the lining is sewn in well. A lining that is crooked or bunchy throws off the line of a garment. You'll either have to rip it out, replace it, or, in the case of a dress or skirt, wear a slip. Calculate whether or not the tailoring will be costly enough that you should just suck it up and spend a bit more on something better made.

▶ **Check the look of any hem:** Cheap skirt and pant hems as well as jacket and coat lapels and cuffs can look heavy and thick. A professional press usually helps flatten things out.

▶ **Prints and stripes:** Patterns and lines should match up where they meet at the seams. If they don't, put it back; it screams *cheap*.

▶ **Is it stiff or supple?** I'm always amazed at the convincing leather and suede designer fakes at Zara and Club Monaco, for example. As I mentioned before, inexpensive skins and cheap wools may have a stiff hand. The softer a fabric or skin looks on your body and the more supple the drape, the more expensive it will look. Squeeze things, walk around, and sit down in things before you buy.

▶ **Look closely at stitching:** On lapels, pockets, the waistband. Is it straight or spotty? Crooked stitches are a dead giveaway. Check buttons too. If they are very cheap plastic, replace them with something more expensive.

trends

Now, let's talk about the big biannual themes that create the excitement in a season and the critical agents of change that keep fashion moving (and keep us shopping). At their well-edited best the latest ideas infuse our wardrobes with glamour, wit, verve, and nerve. But at their over-the-top worst many **head-to-toe** looks can play like an overwrought stage costume, making the average woman look ridiculous.

For starters—*yes, it's my mantra*—choose good, clean design over gimmicks: A sleek coat with a bracelet-length sleeve is a better endorsement of your **style IQ** than a coat with a tortured, tricky construction, a few belts, and a handful of grommets thrown in for good measure (no matter who's designed it, sorry). Witness the hapless *style violators* who wander into the crosshairs of the fashion paparazzi—the poster girls for those "what was she thinking?" columns or the celebrities who bump into the microphones of cable television's so-called fashion experts. Here there's usually too much in one outfit, or too little, and a collision of "creative ideas."

It's the Small Things

Good design employs interesting details—*top stitching or piping along a seam; a delicate pleating or a little shirring or ruching at the neck or shoulder line of a shirt or sweater; a fuller sleeve, an interesting cuff treatment, tonal trim*—often subtle, but they're there. Keep a lookout for the little things—they quietly distinguish a standout basic in a marketplace of the same shapes and colors. Small details add up to a higher style quotient than loud embellishment or color that clubs you over the head with its presence in an outfit. The more elaborate and noticeable the fabric, the more flamboyant the color or pattern, then the cleaner the silhouette should be, and the more precisely cut, to maintain the fragile balance between distinctive style and costume.

Buying Trends

Trends now cycle so quickly that forgotten dry cleaning is considered "vintage." The themes listed here, however, recycle so consistently that we'll call them the *classics* of the trends terrain. They resurface with frequency in new guises because they give designers and us an accessible way to mix pieces, to add contrasts to a look, to expand conventional ideas about masculine and feminine attire, or to add surface interest to an outfit. Invest in any of the following confidently but focus on *fit* and the simple lines that will give them recycling potential and many lives in your closet.

- ▶ **Lace skirt:** In wool or cotton lace, especially in black or an unexpected color like deep brown or ochre, a dressed up and dressed down option in any closet. Pair it as easily with a turtleneck and boots and a leather jacket as with a soft knit top and a sexy heel for cocktails.
- ▶ **Slip dress or slip skirt:** Mixable year-round with textured cardigan sweaters and as soft underpinnings for all weights of tailored or tough jackets and coats.
- ▶ **Camisole:** In soft cotton, silk, and lace, as familiar and useful as a white shirt under jackets or off-the-shoulder sweaters (*see* chapter 6 for bra and shapewear tips).

▶ **The leather jacket:** Like a good handbag, have one with a nipped waist or a refined sport shape with simple lines in black or dark brown so that it can mix with everything you own.

▶ **Army, navy, safari:** A sharp coat or jacket that picks up on the eternal theme of military *cross dressing* for women is virtually timeless, particularly in a classic cut with details that avoid exaggeration (no huge lapels, enormous roll-back cuffs, or platter-sized buttons).

▶ **Sheer tops:** Any unlined, sheer look is only as successful as the artful layering you can cook up for wear underneath. Look for underpinnings that hug and outline your body so that there is absolutely no bulk to throw off the line and the illusory effect. For example, for solid chiffon shirts in pastels or primaries, I'll look for a stretch camisole in a slightly lighter tonal combination for a color-washed effect that doesn't pull focus from the top itself. This uncluttered tactic works under a jacket at the office as well. For casual fabrics like sheer cotton voile, for instance, I like the look of a soft flesh-colored (your skin color) camisole with a lace border that mirrors the sheer color over it. The effect is young, cheeky, your body seen and not seen. When I find the perfect inexpensive flesh camisole or tank, but it is unadorned, I visit a trimmings shop and choose a gorgeous, colorful lace to hand stitch along the straps and neckline for an expensive custom lingerie look. For black, sheer fabrics, try the classic dressed look of either a subtle black stretch lace camisole, or, again, for a younger take, a flesh tone with a black lace trim or overlay. For sheer prints choose either a flesh-toned match or a coordinated dark tone, period.

TIP: The bra-under-sheer thing is passé. It has a kind of *American Idol*-contestant quality that is best avoided. Not to mention the visual miscalculation of slicing your upper body into thirds. Keep the line underneath long, unbroken, and fitted by wearing a stretch camisole with an underwire bra cup built in.

▶ **Metallics:** Include them in your mix to add light, texture, and a day-to-night quality to simple shapes. Good bets for longevity: A skirt in a classic shape like pencil or a slight A-line, a seasonless coat, a fitted jacket, sweater knits, and accessories, of course (more on that in chapter 7). For any metallic, go for a subtle wash of color, a burnished or muted finish rather than their brassier cousins. Again, textured wools shot with metallic thread or sequins are a chic, expensive-looking way to capture the sensibility. Keep the tones understated and they'll pair better with day-to-day staples like jeans, white shirts, and lightweight knits that will give the look its daytime edge.

▶ **Textured knits:** Especially if your wardrobe is primarily solid, the textures you introduce in sweaters, coats, and jackets will break up unrelieved mono or tonal combinations. Substantial, chunky knits are irresistible but potentially very bulky-looking. The more heft to the texture, the more *volume* it will add to your body. Pair your knits with smooth, lightweight wool, silk, linen, or denim. Good bets for all body sizes: vertical, textured patterns and ribs, uniformly small to midsize crochet, small to midsize cables, all-over open weaves.

▶ **Prints:** Buying a trendy print is an easy way to add a bit of current to your closet. Pay attention to the scale and contrast of a print, however. A light pattern on a dark background will always pop and appear larger than a dark print on a light ground. Good bets for all body sizes: midscale prints in tonal color combinations on medium to light-hued grounds, graphic black and white combinations like blown-up houndstooth or geometric patterns.

TIP: If you've ever been stuck with a print or striped bottom of hard-to-match colors and had no better option than white or black tops, take the time to find a compatible top while you have it in hand at the store. Particularly with designer pieces, the colors have been blended and customized for a very distinct look so that it often makes sense to match something from the collection. This is just about the only time your stylist will encourage you to go for a matched option, however.

▶ **Vintage:** While the cachet of authentic, one-of-a-kind clothing is undeniable, shopping for vintage clothes can be hard work unless you have a focus. Don't make the mistake of buying a piece simply because it's an original example of something *au courant* (*unless it's an "It" bag, then of course wrestle any woman to the ground who tries to grab it first*); it should fit well to start or be made of a fabric resilient enough to withstand any needed alterations. The pattern making of yesterday accommodated bodies significantly smaller than the sizing of today. Shop for your shapes in everything just as you would for new clothing and zero in on those decades that cut for your silhouette. Mixing pieces from different decades with compatible sensibilities and shapes can look wonderful but make sure that it all adds up to a silhouette that works for you, not against you. Look for unusual, one-of-a-kind fabrics in dresses that you can have a tailor rework into a better shape. The clearer you are about the shapes that you are going for, the less likely you are to buy something special that sits in your closet. When you do hit pay dirt, especially if you've found an expensive piece you'll keep forever, ask the seller who they use for dry cleaning and for recommended storage specifics.

a few common pitfalls, (or how to avoid the fashion trenches)

BIG LOOKS: It happens every season. Designer looks are launched on the runway and those judged influential for their new perspective on proportion, use of color, or sheer outrageousness, rocket into the fashion stratosphere. We stylists and fashion editors get in line to pull these same few looks for the fashion shoots you'll look at a few months later in the magazines. Seen again and again, by the time you visit your dream looks on the selling floor they've effectively been ground to fashion dust. It's no news to any keen shopper that these same big looks are the first to be interpreted by the teams at fast fashion emporiums like Zara, H&M, Express, Arden B., Mexx, London's Top Shop, and Club Monaco.

Any overexposed look says more about the designer's sensibility and *a moment* in fashion than the woman wearing it and is a look that will be very short-lived. My assistants and I call it *big look syndrome* whenever we see a woman who's wearing a look *to the letter* as it appeared on the runway. If you've clawed your way to the top of the waitlist and you've got to have the real thing, verbatim, it just can't matter to you that you'll see yourself coming and going all over the country. You can't care that you've jumped on a bandwagon instead of doing your own thing. But it should. Think about the look you are going for overall. Nothing has greater appeal and charm than a personal style pulled together from self-expression rather than from a designer's look book.

Log on to **style.com** (as stylists do, constantly) to look at the collection as a whole. Designers always send a few similar looks down the runway in a series of exits. Anyone talented enough to make that much noise on the runway will have a few more less-visible tricks up their sleeve. From these you can choose different colors and fabrics in the same silhouette. Buy the piece that anchors the look and make it your own with a piece of vintage or similar pieces from other sources high or low. This is always the modern and individual approach anyway, and the biggest difference between a woman with personal style and a fashion victim. If you shop for an *interpretation* of the look, as most of us do, go ahead and buy a verbatim knockoff if it looks good on you. Buy it cheap, cheerful, and **fast,** and enjoy it for the five minutes it lasts.

LOGO LUST: Thankfully, fashion has moved beyond the *moment* when wearing a combo platter of status logos in one outfit was considered style and not consumer gluttony. Your stylist implores you to skip any designer logos splashed across your breasts or on a butt pocket. Recently spotted in a posh Fifth Avenue department store, a woman wearing an elaborately embroidered T-shirt proclaiming "J'adore Dior!" Although your stylist shares her enthusiasm for the house of Dior, this would not compel me to wear the enthusiasm on my chest. Ladies, please don't allow yourselves to function as ad hoc billboards for any fashion conglomerate. Indulge any logo lust with extreme subtlety and with accessories. If you love logos, why not slap *your* monogram on something instead?

SEX: There are few other areas of fashion as subjective as dressing to be sexy. So I'll keep this short and sweet. It is probably not a shocker to you, having read this far, that it is your stylist's opinion that the subtle approach to sexy—the velvet hammer versus the sledgehammer—is the way to go. A slice of shoulder, a flash of leg from a side-slit pencil skirt, a sliver-thin high heel, a little cleavage, a strapless dress. You get it. Show a little skin and let your personality and a good fragrance take care of the rest.

I'll give you a comparison of the styles of two designers. In the hands of sexologist Gucci and YSL Rive Gauche designer Tom Ford, sex is bold, strong, confident, and chic (and widely imitated at all price ranges). His ideas are a good template to follow for sexy style with sophistication. Then there is a designer like Roberto Cavalli whose designs speak to the sledgehammer method (also widely imitated at all price ranges). His is a marketable formula of combining over-the top embellishments (a lot of them) with skintight, open-to-the-waist, crotch-high fit for a more-is-more effect. If you are after maximum impact, hope that men will drop things when you walk into a room, then this approach may be your thing, but remember that what looks exciting or provocative enough to pop on the pages of *Us Weekly* or on screen at the MTV Awards can have a *Showgirls* quality in real life.

AGE: Thankfully, age matters less than ever in fashion. But even in a no-rules, wear-whatever-you-want culture, the confusion that women over forty can feel about what they see on the selling floor can be profoundly irritating. When shopping for any woman over thirty-five, I look carefully (again, research) at the collections of Narciso Rodriguez, Calvin Klein, Donna Karan, Carolina Herrera, Michael Kors, Chanel, Celine, Missoni, YSL Rive Gauche, Gucci, and Burberry Prorsum for ideas and individual pieces (budget permitting) that are **ageproof.** Clean lines and smart, sophisticated design always work in any outfit, demonstrating that *age is secondary to an individual sense of style.*

Again, I look everywhere and at all price ranges, as you should, because with a clear focus on your body type and an eye out for current, simple lines, you'll score in unexpected places. I scour the racks of all kinds of stores for things that help me build looks on a kind of fashion timeline. My rule of thumb: the more years lived, the fewer bells and whistles. Tricky details and tortured constructions are the territory of girls in their teens and twenties. By thirty-five, a woman has earned a merit badge or two in smarts and life experience and her wardrobe needs to reflect a confidence that doesn't rely on a lot of gimmicks.

At a certain age we can all experience a case of what I'll call *fashion regression*. It's all too easy to fall in love—again—with a reinterpretation of something you wore the first time (or second or third) it was in style. Revisiting a look that drew raves in your teens or twenties when you are thirty-five or older—especially a very literal take on the idea—can be a recipe for disaster.

I see it every day on the streets of New York: women dressed too young for their age. And please don't say "well, figures, that's New York" because I've also seen this brand of style misstep in my travels all over the country and the world (yes, even in Paris). Not long ago I dressed an actress in her mid-forties. She arrived at the shoot wearing a high-on-the-thigh mini, a pair of eighties redux scrunchie boots, and a black turtleneck. At a few inches above the knee, her skirt would still have displayed plenty of her long legs. It would have been fashionably short for her age and *au courant*. Had she just chucked those Three Musketeers boots (yup, they were big at the moment) for a sleek, knee-high boot, with her turtleneck in place she would have dressed her enviable body to perfection. She would have achieved an **ageproof**, subtly sexy look. Instead, the effect played like a primal scream for validation that she was still young-looking. The problem was not her looks or sex appeal (abundant) but rather her fashion miscalculation.

I see lots of moms who shop for their teenaged daughters and *themselves* in contemporary departments and at stores like Wet Seal. I've seen enough mother-daughter, lowriding, croptopped looks to send my head swiveling. Sadly for mom, the effect is *mutton dressed as lamb* dressed as fashion victim. Mom, just swap those Britney-esque, ultralow riders for a bootcut jean or slim pant with a contoured, low waist and wear them with a sleek boot instead of the platform clogs. Cover that tummy with a cool cotton shirt, a nonlogo T-shirt, or a skimming sweater, and pull in a bit of groovy with a trendy belt or bag. This is a bulletproof approach and you'll have the age thing licked.

a few more tips

Now that we've shopped together—a few more tips.

▶ When it counts, when you really need to get something accomplished, *go shopping alone.* We all love an outing with our girlfriends but they slow us down.

▶ Concentrate on you, your shapes, and try on everything you consider buying in the fitting room. Trust the three-way mirror to get the most realistic, fully dimensional sense of the lines of anything you try on.

▶ Wear a smooth bra and pants or a thong for the best read on anything you try on. If your goal is dresses, evening dresses, skirts, or pants that you know you'll want to wear with a heel, bring the right heel height with you for your most accurate read on the line and proportion. Most good stores have a pair or two of shoes in the dressing room but for the way most of us shop—which is at all kinds of stores—better to be a Girl Scout and arrive prepared.

▶ When you work with a great salesperson take their card, find out their schedule, and seek them out for help with sizes that may not be on the selling floor. They can arrange for any in-store alterations, hold things aside for you, and give you the heads-up on sales.

▶ Never shop when you are hungry or exhausted. Shopping when you're having a physical meltdown is a sure way to make bad choices. Always carry water and a snack if you have a shopping marathon planned.

All right, we've covered some ground together, but one more thing before we move on. Even if you feel that what you see pictured on the runways or in fashion editorials is as relevant to your day-to-day life as kabuki theater, pay attention to what goes on in the stores. Teams of buyers have weeded through all of the calculated runway stunts so by the time you do your own research on the designer floor, **focused only on your silhouette, your proportions, and your lifestyle,** you may be very pleasantly surprised at how relevant many pieces look, and how easily you can adapt them at a price you can afford. But remember, always do your own detective work, take charge of your best fit, and don't rely on magazine pictures or style television to make sense of your style needs. ●

5 your tailor is your new best friend

As a consumer culture we are pretty much defined by our tendency to shake it out of the shopping bag or mail pouch and wear it the very next day. If something you've just bought doesn't fit you perfectly (and really, what are the odds it will?) it is *essential* to tailor it first.

Budget permitting, I always hire a tailor on shoots so that any piece of clothing that moves in front of the camera is truly three-dimensional. Instead of pins and quick stitches, the smooth perfection of a tailored surface means clothing looks beautiful from any angle. The model moves with ease and confidence. Make this your experience in clothes. Finding perfect fit in mass manufactured clothing gets tougher all the time. If there are no ticks or bumps to sort out before a first wearing, you have beaten the odds but this doesn't happen often.

You can generally have a serviceable hem let up or down right at your local dry cleaner. Most large department stores offer tailoring services free of charge and will only charge you for sale merchandise that needs repairs, for example. Specialty stores like Banana Republic and J.Crew offer the basics: lengthening and shortening, cuffs and waist adjustments. When it comes to the alterations that transform something from passable to perfection on your body you need a very good tailor. A relationship with a talented tailor is like finding a great hairstylist: a professional who understands when to trim away a little and how to change the shape altogether. My relationship with my long-time tailors is three parts collaboration and one part psychiatry.

how to find a good tailor

Ask friends. Failing a good recommendation there, scan the *Yellow Pages*, as you would hunt for any other business. Browse the Internet by entering *custom tailoring* into a search engine. Be sure to specify your city or town. Here are the key services you are looking for from a tailor: ***alterations, custom tailoring, repairing,*** and ***restyling.*** When trying to sort out which tailor to try, here's a tip. Any tailor that advertises that they make custom menswear is the person you want to investigate first. Call and talk with them to be certain they offer alterations for women as well. The tailor who is skilled with menswear constructions and fabrics is your best bet for the most complicated women's clothing alterations.

If you can't find a tailor in your area, research your local dry cleaners. Ask them what tailoring services they offer. You want a dry cleaner who has a tailor on site. What you don't want is the proprietor of the store leaving the cash register to throw a few pins in your clothes only to send them out to an independent contractor. If they do send things out, however, ask to whom. If the person or service is local, track them down. Call and ask to schedule an appointment. The most successful alterations require that the tailor do the pinning, feel the fabric, and look at the proportions of your body in the construction.

If there are no tailors on site at your dry cleaner and no independent tailoring shops in your area, call a local bridal shop. Ask if they send out any of their tailoring work and, if so, to whom. Another tip: most bridal shops have a staff tailor or seamstress who makes and alters custom bridesmaid dresses. Often, these tailors or seamstresses do a bit of freelancing at home. Be brassy and ask.

As you try any new tailor, start small. Bring them a simple hem or waist alteration for example. When you pick up your clothing, always try things on to make sure that the work is a success. Does the hem fall well? Is the drape the same? Have a look at the quality of the stitches. They should be small, uniform, secure. Does every inch of the garment look *smooth*? Be certain that the lining of the garment isn't caught up or bunching along a seam.

If you've found a good tailor, none of these things will come up. If you are satisfied with the work, move on to something more complicated the next time like taking in a jacket, for example. If you are less than thrilled with the results, be vocal and specific about what looks wrong to your eye and ask the tailor to correct the problem. Any additional tweaks should always be free of charge.

To get the most from your tailor, it's a good idea to have at least a passing understanding of what can be done to improve the fit of your clothes. It helps to talk with him or her articulately about how you want the end result to look. Do not hesitate to ask the tailor questions about how a problem can be remedied. That said, here's a head start to demystify a process that a lot of women have told me they've never investigated because they don't know what to ask for, they assume it will be astronomically expensive, or they are afraid that the tailor might ruin something expensive.

advice from the experts

I ran a checklist of the most frequent problems we girls (at all sizes) encounter with fit and how your tailor should best remedy them with two behind-the-scenes tailoring wizards, Lars Nord and Monica Willis. Lars' tailoring talents are in demand on the sets of shoots for Versace, Ralph Lauren, Abercrombie & Fitch, and Calvin Klein, to name a few, and Monica is a costume designer for films, videos, and advertising. Their custom work has saved my bacon on many a shoot. Here's some of their general advice:

▶ **For any alterations, always give your tailor enough fabric to work with.** *Never* buy something too small thinking it can be let out. The seam allowance for most garments will accommodate an addition of no more than a quarter inch in total. Not nearly enough for most of us. Always go up a size. Fabric to a tailor is literally like clay to a sculptor. Your tailor can mold and shape your clothes based on the amount and quality of the fabric he or she has to work with.

> **TIP:** A possible exception: If something is vintage, very special, and all you need is *less than an inch* of grace, the good news is that vintage clothing (before mass manufacturing) often has a more generous seam allowance. Turn a garment inside out and have a look at the seams. Gauge how much you have to play with before you spend your money.

▶ **Always bring your tailor clean clothes.** Tailors press the fabric while they work (sometimes repeatedly during the course of an alteration). You may end up with a perfectly tailored garment with a stain made indelible by the heat of the press.

▶ **Always give your tailor the most accurate sense of your body in the garment** by wearing a smooth bra and panties along with any specific foundation pieces you'll need to achieve the smoothest fit. For example, a strapless long-line bra can be stitched into a strapless dress for the optimum, molding fit. Have the right shoes with you to achieve an accurate hem length.

Specifics

▶ **Waists:** Girls, never suck in your stomach when a tailor is taking in a waistband. Your tailor shouldn't hold the measuring tape too tightly, flush to your skin. Ask your tailor to hold the tape a bit loose for a little built-in ease (or insert two fingers under the waist band as the tailor is pinning). Ideally, schedule a fitting after lunch when your body fluids have settled a bit to achieve the most realistic and flattering fit.

▶ **Hems:** All hems on fine fabrics should be done by hand for the smoothest surfaces and the best drape and fall.

> **TIP:** Exceptions to the rule are alterations on any garment that has been topstitched by machine to begin with, that is, denim jeans, khakis, cotton pants, cotton shirts.

pants

A pant should always *suggest* the shape of your leg (except, of course, a very wide leg). It doesn't matter if your legs are small, medium, or large. A smooth, skimming fit in the right cut for your shape, with a hem length that brushes the toe of your shoe, will make your legs look longer and sleeker. Here's how we get there.

▶ **Shaping the leg:** Following the line of the garment, your tailor should reduce the width of the entire leg by taking away fabric from both the outer seam and the inseam to achieve the most balanced proportion. This is good news when you want to *restyle* a wide-leg trouser to a stovepipe or bootcut, for example.

▶ **Baggy bottom:** If you've got a little bagging through the bottom, it's an easy fix. Your tailor will remove the excess fabric through the center back seam to create smoothness.

▶ **Baggy under the center back waistband:** We've all had a pair of these—especially pants with a lot of stretch in the fabric; even

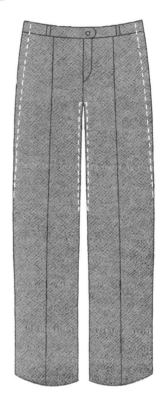

with a belt, there's a bunchy ridge of excess fabric under the waistband. This happens because the pant seat is cut too long for your waist-to-bottom length. Your tailor will remedy the problem by removing the waistband, cutting away the excess length, and re-attaching the waistband.

▶ **Rise is too long:** A particular problem for petites. This can be a big job depending on the style of the pant. Jeans, forget it. For good wool pants, though, your tailor can usually remove up to one inch. Beyond an inch and you might as well recut a new pant. The most successful style for rise reductions: Smooth styles with a back or side zipper and no pocket details that sit too close to the waistband. Since the waistband must be removed to allow for the removal of the excess length, any pockets that sit too close will have to be cut down as well, thus throwing off the line of the garment entirely.

▶ **Excess in the hips:** They fit otherwise except for the *airbags* of excess fabric through the hip. Instead of cursing the manufacturer's fit model, ask your tailor to shave away the excess on the outer seam from the waistband to low hip.

> **TIP:** Your tailor should remove the excess out of a straight skirt that has a bell shape in the same way.

▶ **Commit to a length:** Bring shoes of the heel height you've chosen. This is one area in which we can't have it all. If you want them long enough to brush the top of your shoe in heels, you can't mop the floor with them the next day in a pair of ballet flats. Shoe-grazing lengths look slouchy, a hem dragging on the ground is just plain sloppy.

skirts

Just as with a pair of pants, your tailor will follow the line of the garment at the outer seams to narrow the width. A bias-cut skirt, with fabric sewn on the diagonal, can be a trickier skirt to take in. Done badly and the side seams will ripple. In any pant or skirt made of lightweight fabrics like jersey, washed silk, or thin cotton if you constantly fight panty lines or clinging (and you wear smooth pants that don't budge from your bottom, more on this in chapter 6) consider having your tailor add a lightweight half lining (for pants) or a full lining (for skirts, dresses).

jackets

▶ **Nip the waist:** To create a fluid, shapely line, your tailor should pin from below your breast and along the length of your rib cage at the outer seam. Working with the specific cut of the jacket, any seaming or darts, he'll follow your silhouette to create a skimming shape that eliminates any excess through your torso. A coatdress is tailored in the same way.

- ▶ **Shortening a jacket:** Only works as a slight length adjustment and only when the proportion overall is right for your size. For example, petite women of any size should not alter a garment sized for a taller proportion and expect the best possible fit. Shortening alone can't balance everything else—pockets that sit too low, buttons that start below bust level, a back vent that disappears with the excess length. For a petite woman, it's always best to buy clothes that are cut specifically for your proportions.

> **TIP:** Just as when you try on a jacket in a store, wear the right weight top and that everyday, smooth bra underneath to achieve the most accurate alterations and fit.

- ▶ **Neck, shoulders, and sleeves:** Often when a jacket is big through the body it also requires pulling in the shoulder line (so that the seams meet the edge of your shoulders); narrowing the collar so that it molds to your neck (removing excess down the center back seam); and narrowing and shortening the sleeves (removing the excess down the center back sleeve of the seam). Essential for good jacket fit: the volume of the entire jacket is balanced, symmetrical, plumb.
- ▶ **The lining:** Never let a small tear or opening in a lining become a big one. Aside from looking grubby, this puts stress on the garment from within. This will also separate a small mending job from a potentially big (and expensive) lining replacement.

shirts

Button-front shirts in cotton or silk can benefit from a nip and tuck.

▶ **Through the torso:** Any button-front cotton shirt with a boxy fit that hides your shape should be pulled out of your closet and taken to the tailor. Shirts can easily be trimmed in through the torso, along the side seams, to achieve a balanced, skimming line.

▶ **Shirt hem and cuffs:** Especially helpful for girls who wear a lot of men's shirts and for short-waisted petites. If a shirt is too long it is easy to shorten and to duplicate the original line of the hem. Arms can be narrowed slightly and shortened, the shirt cuff removed and reattached.

dresses

A dress is one of the easiest things to tailor or recut into a different shape altogether. I've watched Lars alter the shapes of things as complicated and unconventional as a Versace metal mesh evening gown and as fragile as an intricately beaded Prada satin sheath. Monica has transformed many shapeless vintage dresses made of gorgeous fabric into sleek, skimming silhouettes.

▶ **Shape:** It's a snap for your tailor to install a nip in the waist of a stick-straight dress. With enough fabric a dress can be recut and reshaped entirely.

▶ **Gapping through the bust:** Often happens when the armhole is too large causing the fabric between the arm and bust to bag and buckle. With a lot of bagging, especially for sleeveless styles, the best solution is to have your tailor recut the armhole. The placement of a simple dart through the bust does the trick.

▶ **One more thought:** Bringing a very inexpensive piece of tailored clothing like a jacket or coat to a tailor and expecting fit miracles is unrealistic. If the full price is very low to start, the low price has been made possible by cheap materials and cheap labor. Have it professionally pressed instead and hope that the fabric is stable enough to maintain a good pressing, and that the seams will smooth out and look flat. If not, take it back, and don't waste money on tailoring.

custom-made clothing

Ask yourself how many times you have said "if this just came in my size" or "I would love this in a different color" or with a lower neckline, a longer sleeve, and so on? What we've gained in the convenience and instant gratification of ready-to-wear, we've lost in the principles of the dressmaking art, where patterns were created to the specifications of one woman's individual measurements. Numerous fittings assured her an ideal proportion and the most flattering silhouettes for her body. For the very wealthy, this is one obvious allure of couture clothing.

Custom-made clothing is the stylist's secret weapon and it can be yours too. If I can't find the right shape, color, or size for a shoot or for a private client, I have it made. I scout the racks, as usual, in all kinds of stores and when I find a great shape in something I take it straight to Lars or Monica to be duplicated. (Yes, I return it to the store, tags in place, and in perfect condition when the work is done.) If you have a difficult time finding flattering shapes in the fabrics you want, have them made. The combined cost of labor and fabric is often half what you would pay for a comparable designer piece of clothing at retail.

Here's one example of how custom saves the day and is neither complicated nor too costly: Before the debut of her eponymous clothing line, Emme was awarded a contract with Revlon as their first full-fashion spokesmodel. I was hired to style looks for her appearances in print ads, in television commercials, and personal appearances. Truthfully, my assignments up until this point had seldom necessitated anything over a size 6. What I found was a less than limited range of options. Where were the sexy shaped dresses? Where were the pencil skirts and current-looking pants? With the help of a talented tailor, we created these pieces. Here are some ideas that can work for you too—at any size.

copycats

Good tailors can create a pattern based on any article of clothing you bring them. It doesn't have to be your size exactly—it should be close—and the tailor will factor in your measurements to accommodate the difference. What works best of course, is to bring a tailor your best-fitting items, be it a pant, skirt, dress, or suit, and have them copied exactly. Always try it on so they can look at your proportions in the garment, assess the fit, and talk with you about how you may improve on things further with a little off here and a little added there. The end result will require further fittings, as a good tailor will always leave a little extra room so that the last tweaks will create the ideal skimming fit over your body. In fact, you should ask them to do this to be sure you'll achieve a perfect end result.

If you can't find a good tailor in your area, you can try an online service for pants and skirts called **AmericanFit.com** (201-653-9466). They offer a basic range of styles including a clean-front pant, a trouser skirt, and a pencil skirt, along with denim jeans. They can accommodate any size and their policy is simple. Either fit yourself following their checklist of requested measurements, or send them your pants or skirt for duplication. The catch is that you are limited to their fabric selection, which is small and very basic. They do offer a standard tropical-weight black wool and black leather.

finding good ready-to-wear fabrics

Fabric is critical for the success of any custom-made copy. Choose a fabric with a hand (the same feel, weight, and drape, stretch or nonstretch) that is as close as possible to the original piece. Remember that the fabric for the original has been chosen by the designer and manufacturer to support the construction. It's best to follow their lead if you want to duplicate the look and achieve the best fit. For example, if a pant is made of tropical wool with soft drape, you may be very disappointed with the same construction in cotton or denim. When you shop for fabric in a store, always have the original with you. Ask for advice on comparable options.

Your stylist is very aware that some parts of the country simply do not have a wide selection of ready-to-wear fabric stores, if any. While the offerings online are improving, let me save you a whole lot of time. Fortunately, two of Seventh Avenue's very best fabric and notion resources are now available for Internet shopping:

▶ **B & J Fabrics** (bandjfabrics.com or 866-354-8150): The first place your stylist goes for any custom sewing project. A vast selection of all kinds of fine fabrics including end of the season leftovers (known as *mill ends* in the biz) from Seventh Avenue's finest designers. The store also buys fabrics directly from European mills that supply fabrics to Chanel and Valentino, to name but two. From fabrics with a right-off-the-runway look to timeless weaves, this store has it all. The selection of cotton includes the full catalog of prints from Liberty of London. B & J also offers a swatching service. Call them directly and describe what you are looking for as specifically as possible and they will snip and send you options to review. Again, I'll stress, you have to be specific or send them an example of the color and fabric you are looking for and they'll send you the most appropriate matches at no charge.

▶ **M & J Trimmings** (mjtrim.com or 212-391-6200): The right buttons and trims are critical to the finished appearance of a piece. Log on to this site for a vast assortment of notions. M & J also offers a swatching service on any trim that is sold by the yard. The store will snip a 3″ swatch at a cost of $4 to $7 per cut. The cost of your swatches is deducted from the cost of your order.

Also try **Fabric.com**, **Fashionfabricsonline.com**, and **ebay.com**: This is hit or miss but sellers often auction various lots of beautiful ready-to-wear yardage, new and vintage, priced to sell. Ebay is a treasure hunt, for sure, but it is well worth browsing to unearth something unique.

bring your tailor a pattern

A pattern is particularly handy when you just can't find a good example in the stores. Choose a pattern for a clean flat-front pant, a straight, A-line or pencil skirt, then spin it out in different fabrics, lengths, and seam or hem trimmings to change the look. Here's what I mean.

For Emme's Revlon wardrobe, for example, I chose a pattern for a straight skirt from *Vogue* Patterns, *Vogue* Woman Collection. Monica Willis adapted it easily to the perfect shape by narrowing the skirt gradually from hip to hem for a just-below-the-knee length. Black, camel, and charcoal skirts filled in the gaps for three current-looking, indispensable bottoms. Later, for different magazine shoots, we revived this same pattern for an ankle length, deeply side slit number in lime green sequins worn with a crisp white shirt for what was at that moment a right-off-the-runway look. Two more variations on the knee length theme included a curvaceous Chinese brocade and a stretch wool with diagonally placed hand beading (from M & J, of course). One silhouette and two proportions provided endless possibilities. I found all of these fabric options at B & J Fabrics. When something works and looks current, have it made indefinitely from season to season.

For patterns online try: mccall.com: All patterns specifiy petite, average missy, and woman sizing. A tip for full-fashion girls: Look at the patterns for flat-front pants, pencil skirts, and classic dresses (perfect in matte jersey) from Vogue Patterns, Today's Fit by Sandra Betzina.

I seldom style a cosmetics advertising job without having at least a few things knocked off in the exact colors or shapes I can't find in the stores. In my own life, I can seldom find pants long enough in the rise, or to accommodate my thirty-six-inch inseam. When I find a good pant from which to make a pattern, I have two or three more made in different colors. The advantage? Perfect fit because they are made on my body. Better yet, they cost roughly half of any designer pant. As I mentioned before when we cleaned out your closet, hang on to current but road-weary pieces and use them for patterns.

TIP: If you have trouble finding good belts in your size, have them made. Sash belts and obis in very soft leather, suede, velvet ,or brocades are easy for a tailor to run up on the sewing machine. Bring an example of what you want copied and ask your tailor what his machines can accommodate. Having an obi or wraparound sash made in the same fabric as a dark skirt can give you an option to finish your waist, and change the look for day and night.

restyles

I'll remind you again that any designer pieces you'd like to tweak should be brought out of the closet. Talk with your tailor about your options for restyling such things as a dress to a top or tunic, a jacket to a vest, a coat to a belted jacket. Shorten and reshape last year's trendy long skirt. If you've invested in good design and fabric in the first place you can often give things a new look and a new life in your closet.

Reweaving and repairs: You cannot count on your dry cleaner to offer sophisticated reweaving and repair services for serious tears in good fabrics, leathers, or tears and holes in knits. If you cannot find a service in your area that specifically offers these services log on to **withoutatrace.com** or call 800-475-4922 for reweaving for fine knitwear, wool, and repairs and conditioning for leather, suede, shearling, and fur. Send them the item in question with a request for an estimate on the labor.

Furs and shearling coats that look dated but that represent a considerable investment can be restyled into current looks. If you can't find someone in your area, try **furcenter.com**. The Web site will route you to a specialist furrier near you. The network includes over fifty stores, and inspections are free. The specialist will provide you with an estimate on the labor based on the condition of the piece and of course, the complexity of what you want done to change the look.

what it will cost

Costs for altering or constructing tailored clothing can vary significantly from city to suburbs. You've always got to consider your tailor's location and how much rent he pays! These costs are passed on to you. Here is a ballpark average of prices for common alterations based on a sampling of businesses in major cites and large suburbs alike, from both coasts and the middle of the country.

Pant Hems
- $12.00 by hand
- $8.00 by machine
- $15.00 with cuffs

Shirt Hems and Cuffs
- $15.00 by hand
- $10.00 by machine
- $15.00 cuffs shortened

Waists
- $12.00

Seam Repairs
- $2.00 and up

Zippers Replaced
- $10.00
- $12.00 with fly front

Skirts or Pants
- $15.00 and up

Lining Repairs for Jackets and Coats
- $20.00 and up

Lining Replacements for Jackets and Coats
- $50.00 and up

custom costs

Custom clothing costs vary wildly depending on the experience and reputation of the tailor, location (as I mentioned), and their clientele (prices that reflect what the traffic will bear).

Here is a big-city average. These same services can cost as little as half in suburban areas. Final costs are always dependant on the complexity of the construction, the length, the requested details, the delicacy of the fabric. You must also factor in what you pay for the yardage needed for the piece.

Pants
- $200.00 and up

Daytime skirt
- $150.00 and up

Daytime dresses
- $200.00 and up

Jackets
- $300.00 and up

Coats
- $500.00 and up

Suit
- $600.00 and up

The best comparison to think of here is the difference between what you would pay full price for a piece of a designer's collection clothing versus their bridge line. The distinct advantage, of course, is that it has been made on your body, in fabric with a quality, color, and texture of your choice. The end result is a piece of designer quality for half the price of designer.

I'll mention this again (yes, I'll undoubtedly mention this a few more times before we're finished): The universal truth about women with great personal style is that their clothes really fit; fit to create the longest, smoothest, optimum unbroken line. **This is the key.** This is the beginning of the conversation. You can add lavish accessories to a look but you are throwing good money after bad if they are combined with something that doesn't fit your body. You really don't need a lot to create a great wardrobe. But everything that hangs in your closet should fit, or it is money wasted.

6 what lies beneath

Behind every gorgeous fashion image is a collaboration among wardrobe, hair, makeup, and art direction that results in a picture in which all these independent elements relate well to each other. To create an image that is both distinctive and balanced, not only must the proportions of the clothes suit the model's body, but the foundations—*what lies beneath*—must fit her body perfectly as well. The right bras, panties, and shapewear help *create* the fit. Not all models are perfectly proportioned, by the way. They are not churned out on an assembly line. It only appears that way because of all kinds of subtle *balance illusions* that take place in the dressing room.

Hair styling must also create a balanced *frame* for the shape of the model's face and suit her height and silhouette. Makeup must accentuate rather than overwhelm her facial structure. Well-defined brows are an essential finish for the face. All these elements are critical to creating the total image and *real life is no different.*

If a woman's hairstyle hasn't changed in years or her hair color is wrong for her skin tone, her overall look will be thrown off by the time warp, even with an investment in new and up-to-the-minute clothing. Heavy makeup and overplucked brows detract from the natural balance and beauty in a face. Chipped nail polish and ragged cuticles create a negative focal point at your hands and feet. If just one of these elements in a picture is somehow off, the look won't communicate the right image. *Your life is no different.* Just as you're training your eye for your best shapes and proportions in clothes, your hair and makeup should always help you achieve a balanced, subtly enhanced appearance.

Imagine that you are the subject of a full-length photograph: The goal of the styling and beauty team would not be to transform you into a facsimile of a fashion model but rather to enhance—*amplify,* shall we say—your natural appearance. To create a picture that would represent you at your very best. Here's how your sitting would go.

First, we'd spend time together in wardrobe combing through racks of clothing and picking out styles that worked for you in all the ways we have been talking about. We'd choose clothing for your frame, your proportions, and your skin tone. Equally important, we'd sort out *exactly* the right bra to fit and flatter your natural shape, what shape underpants would give you the smoothest line possible, and the selection of any shapewear to optimize your silhouette.

bras: the right fit and silhouette

For now, let's concentrate on bras. Bra fit is another very big deal in your bag of tricks since your overall presentation is only as successful as the smooth line you create underneath your clothes. Even if you know (or think you know) your correct size, it doesn't mean you have necessarily found the right fit.

Make a point to be properly measured at a lingerie store or take out your tape measure *one more time* (if you have been a Girl Scout, you've already taken these measurements in chapter 1). Follow this **standard formula** used by stores and manufacturers alike.

These measurements, at the very least, will put you in the right series of racks in a department store but if you have never shopped for bras at a lingerie store, I recommend this approach for focused and knowledgeable advice.

Finding great fit in a bra is like finding great fit in a pair of jeans— you have to fill your arms with options and park yourself in front of a mirror in the fitting room. No wonder statistics indicate that up to 80 percent of women wear the wrong size bra. The constructions from manufacturers can vary as widely as the breasts meant to fill them.

If it seems as though every woman should be issued an owner's manual for her breasts, then Rebecca Apsan, owner of La Petite Coquette in New York City, could be the author. Years ago, I wandered into La Petite Coquette, a destination for movie stars, models, and lingerie-loving girls from all over the country. At the

How to Measure Your Bra Size

Braless, and in your underpants please, hold your tape measure directly under your bust and measure around your chest. This number determines your band size.

- If the number is odd, add 5
- If the number is even, add 6
- If the number is over 33″, add 3

Next, hold your tape around the fullest part of your breasts to measure your **cup size.** Subtract your band size from your cup size, and if the difference is:

- 0 = AA
- 1 = A
- 2 = B
- 3 = C
- 4 = D
- 5 = DD
- 6 = DDD

time, I was a fledgling fashion assistant with a history of bralessness and bad cotton underpants and, in the midst of the lushest lingerie imaginable, Rebecca performed my first bra fitting. I should tell you that a fitting with Rebecca is a veritable master class in breast presentation. Here are her tips—I have used them in the dressing room ever since.

▶ **When you try on a bra:** Lean forward and place your breasts into the cups, push them from the side to the center of the cup and hook the back. Adjust the straps so that your breasts are centered and the line looks natural.

▶ **Put a bra back if:**

1. **Your breasts spill over the sides:** Increase your band and/or cup size.

2. **The cups wrinkle or pucker:** Try a different style or a smaller cup. Try a demicup rather than a fuller-cut cup for a better fit and a natural-looking shape.

3. **The bra rides up in the back:** The band is probably too large. Any band should cross the center of your back and stay there to fit securely. Try a smaller band size.

4. **It gaps at the top of the cup or the underwire is not flush to your rib cage.**
5. **Your two breasts are pushed together into one sausage-shaped breast.** Don't wear your sport bra under your clothing if your want a sleek look. Try an underwire for more definition.

For work I carry a lingerie kit contained in a mesh tote the size of a small refrigerator. Why? For one reason, every woman's breasts are a bit different in shape, even if they share the same measurements. Yes, *models too.* My bag—ad hoc lingerie minimart—is filled with dozens of Ziplocs filled with dozens more bras organized by cup size. Why so many? A girl with a small B cup may wear a 34B in one bra style and a 36A in another. It all depends on the construction of the cup and what the bra is meant to do under clothing. Girls with fuller breasts often need to try a series of cup constructions to arrive at the magic bullet for fit, support, and the most natural shape.

There are things you can always tell right on the hanger—for instance, are the cups placed too close together or spaced too far apart for the shape and spacing of your breasts? Is the band of the bra too thin to support the width of your back? Is there seaming across the cup or any applied lace or ribbon prominent enough to look bumpy under clothing? The rest of the fit should be worked out in front of a mirror under the clothing the bra is meant to complement.

> **TIP:** Yes, this often necessitates buying and returning bras, so that you can go through your closet and make sure you have the right shape and fit for everything from cotton tees to a strapless dress. Keep the tags on and organize any receipts so that returns are smooth going at the store.

Here's a checklist of the *indispensable bras* I carry in my kit and that every girl needs in her lingerie drawer:

YOUR EVERYDAY BRA—a smooth cup, no seams, no details, nude bra: For small and fuller breasts alike, *especially under something telling like a T-shirt or a thin sweater*—I like the shape created by smooth, molded cup bras. Molded cups don't increase size but they do create a rounder-looking, more symmetrical bust line. A *molded cup* is actually just that—a metal cup over which fabric is heat transferred. It's cut and sewn into a bra and can be very thin or transparent. *Especially if your breasts hang south, point north, or east and west*, a molded underwire will center your bustline. This is the beginning construction of many of the best bras out there from enhancers to minimizers. My recommended favorites straight from my kit bag:

A/B Cups:
- **On Gossamer**—Bump It Up and 24/7 bras
- **Wonderbra**—Stretch Foam Demi
- **Victoria's Secret**—Angels Collection Stretch Lined Demi
- **Calvin Klein**—Perfectly Fit Demi
- **Jockey**—Demi Cup Enhancer
- **Playtex**—Thank Goodness It Fits, seamless padded cup half-size bras for girls between A and B cups
- **Wolford Body Culture** (these babies are pricey—the Formula One race car of molded constructions)
- **Gap Body**—T-shirt and flawless styles

C/D Cups:
- **Chantelle**—Seamless Minimizer 2065
- **On Gossamer**—24/7
- **Donna Karan Intimates**—Body Smooth Underwire 353
- **Victoria's Secret**—T-shirt bra
- **Victoria's Secret**—Hidden-wire
- **Body by Bali**—Support Stretch Foam Seamless Underwire
- **Playtex**—Thank Goodness It Fits, seamless smooth cups, half-sizes between C and D.
- **Jockey**—Smooth Contours Underwire 1734
- **Gap Body**—Supreme Fit Seamless Underwire

Minimizers for D and larger:
- **Chantelle**—Seamfree Minimizer 2065 (sizes up to G)
- **Le Mystere**—Renaissance Minimizer
- **Bali**—Soothing Spa Strap 3382, 3710
- **Bali**—Underwire Concealers

- **Victoria's Secret**—Emma Collection, full-figure bras
- **Curvations**—sold at Walmart
- **Lane Bryant**—Cacique, their private label bra
- **Gap Body**—Supreme Fit Seamless Underwire

CONVERTIBLE BRA: Again, a smooth, molded, or slightly padded cup and an underwire construction (have one in nude) will serve you well. This is the bra that covers your options in strapless, halters, and one-shoulder tops or dresses. Look for styles that have thin strips of silicone along the band. As the silicone reacts with the heat of your body it forms a no-slip surface against your skin. Another tip: if your bra of choice doesn't come with clear silicone straps, buy a package of clear straps to attach whenever you need near-invisible security.

A/B Cups:
- **On Gossamer**—Mesh convertible
- **Le Mystere**—L'Image Strapless Push Up
- **Wacoal**—convertible bra
- **Maidenform**—One Fabulous Fit convertible bra
- **Fashion Forms**—Ultimate Convertible Bra
- **Victoria's Secret**—Body by Victoria strapless convertible

C/D Cups:
- **On Gossamer**—Mesh Convertible
- **Donna Karan Intimates**—Body Smooth Convertible
- **Victoria's Secret**—Body by Victoria strapless convertible

D and larger cups (long line convertibles are ideal for shaping and support)**:** Look for styles from:
- **Chantelle**
- **Le Mystere**
- **Lane Bryant**—Cacique 5 Convertible seamless long line bra
- **Curvations at Walmart**—long line convertible

Clear straps:
- **Fashion Forms**—department stores or fashionforms.com

TIP: Consider having a smooth nude or black longline convertible on hand specifically for strapless dresses. If you worry about slippage in something strapless, have a tailor baste the right bra into the dress.

BRA-TOP CAMISOLE: In your skin tone, and in black. Choose lightweight mesh with either underwire or a shelf of elastic at the bottom of a panel sewn in for shape, and adjustable bra straps to perfect the fit. This is the piece that disappears under silk and sheer shirts and gives your torso a smooth line in lightweight knits.

perfect panties

Your stylist encourages you to find your ideal panty fit and to fill your drawers with the right panties. Your pants should smooth you out completely with no lines whatsoever, and be *budgeproof* where your cheeks meet your leg.

THONGS: From a fashion perspective, we have been in a thong-centric place for years now, as thongs and G-strings are promoted as the panacea for all pantyline woes. While they do eliminate lines, they can accentuate other problems.

If you have visible cellulite on your booty (like a woman I walked behind down Fifth Avenue recently), *PLEASE* don't wear a thong under a clingy jersey knit skirt. Trust me, the lack of a panty line hardly compensated for the undisguised cottage cheese across her bottom. Her skirt, riding low on her hips, revealed a full view of the top of her thong creating a veritable *high-beam* on the least attractive area of her body.

> **TIP:** Make sure that any thong you choose has the right length rise for you. This is key to a comfortable and smooth fit.

Now, will someone please explain to me why thong exposure has become a sort of *one-two punch* in low-riding waistlines and why any girl past high school wants to look like this? I can understand the kind of naughty, rebel appeal this may have for a sixteen-year-old, but grownup girls should raise the bar. Ladies, remember the eye is immediately drawn to the floss effect of an exposed thong in jeans or a skirt. For any piece of hipriding clothing, at least choose a low rider thong to avoid adding to the visual distraction. Even if—especially if—your bottom is world class this is not, shall we say, as *refined* a presentation as a girl might choose for herself on the street. Sorry, don't care who you've seen photographed with her thong fully exposed. We are after style, and a line for your clothing, and this look doesn't cut it.

Thong alternatives (comfortable and plenty sassy-looking, besides)
- **Cosabella**—mesh hipster boy-leg briefs
- **Mary Green**—silk hipster boy shorts
- **Jockey**—Hipsters, briefs, and bikinis that live up to the no panty line promise on the label. They don't move and they are ultralight. Your stylist is a convert.
- **Chantelle**—stretch boy-leg pants
- **Victoria's Secret**—No Show hiphugger briefs
- **Victoria's Secret**—Body by Victoria low rise boy shorts, hipster, and high-cut brief
- **Gap Body**—sheer hipster
- **Lane Bryant**—Cacique briefs

SILKIES: Add a silky, short, above-the-knee full slip and a few silk camisoles and tap pants to your drawers, as well, for a soft, linefree presentation under sweaters and skirts, for starters.

> **TIP:** Wash all these things in a lingerie bag or by hand in cold water and air dry. Never put an underwire bra in the dryer.

hosiery

Here is your stylist's take on the hosiery issue. Yes, magazines and designers promote a bare-legged look with clothes because it is has a clean, uncomplicated appeal. Regardless of the images you see in magazines, however, you are the best and only judge of what best flatters your legs and your lifestyle. If your office dress code requires hosiery, there are options that will give you a convincingly bare look without the literal translation.

ULTRASHEER: Always choose an ultrasheer leg that is an *exact* match to your natural skin tone. Unless you are a healthcare worker, never go lighter and never wear cream or white stockings. A more unflattering look has never been devised. Donna Karan Hosiery, The Nudes line was one of the first to introduce an ultrasheer collection in a range of very cosmetic and convincing skin-toned matches and it remains one of the very best. The line includes a toeless style to wear with open toe pumps or sandals, but in my opinion, this look never quite comes off. If you have to wear hosiery, opt for closed toe shoes to keep the look convincing and current.

More suggestions for sheer
- **Donna Karan Hosiery**—The Ultimate Sheer Collection
- **Wolford-Le9**—pricey but worth it for a near-invisible finish
- **Fogal**—110 Noblesse
- **Oroblu**—Repos 70
- **Calvin Klein**—number 10 Denier, ultrasheer (try the zero waistband style if you don't need a control top)
- **DKNY SKIN**
- **Victoria's Secret Body Bare**—7 Denier (available in a hipster style)
- **Bloomingdale's**—Silk Sensations (up to Woman 3X)
- **Donna Karan The Nudes** (available in plus and petite plus)

THE RIGHT WAISTBAND: Consider the waistbands on your work skirts from low waist to conventional navel-high styles and be prepared with a few pairs of low-waisted stockings in your stash. Rolling down the waistband on a pair of waist-high hose to wear with a low-waisted skirt creates a *visible* horizontal line under the fabric and, overall, a lumpy effect.

SHEEN: Keep it to a minimum in the daytime for the most natural (and modern) effect.

PATTERNS, TEXTURES: Add volume to the surface of your legs. Aside from what can be a somewhat leg- and knee-thickening effect for many girls, decide whether or not you want your stockings to be the focal point of your look. I'm not a fan of complicated patterns and textures for day, for this reason: to my eye, they always compete with, rather than complement, an outfit. Keep textures smaller or woven with an overall uniformity, like a fishnet in black or camel, or a small-scaled crochet and subtle vertical ribs for the sleekest, leg-lengthening effect. Those dramatic couture laces and overscale geometrics that walk the runways can look fantastic and eye-catching for evening with all black and (yes, life is not fair) on very thin legs.

TIP: Never wear a **bold** textured stocking with an ankle-strap shoe. Your legs become a geometry exercise in diagonal, vertical, and horizontal lines and the effect is unflattering and too busy to look stylish and modern. Keep your legs bare, or bare-looking or wear tights.

OPAQUE TIGHTS: Black tights are universally beloved for an instant dose of chic and for their slimming effect. Nothing looks better with a stiletto pump, a boot, or a colorful shoe than the leggy cool of a matte black leg. During those fashion moments when colored tights are a part of the seasonal trend landscape consider this: this is a look for women under thirty and, if you are one, don't break up your body into blocks of color. If you wear a colored tight it should be subtle and a tonal continuation of your skirt that blends into your shoe or boot to keep the look long-looking and sophisticated, not costumed.

shapewear and other illusions straight from the kit bag

Any piece of shapewear should move with your body: no ride up, no squeezing, no pinching or rolls at any openings. Never buy anything that makes you (painfully) aware that you are wearing it because you are forced to tug or pull on it to keep things together. Ultimately, if you feel inhibited by the sensation of something against your skin, it will affect your body *and* your head. Any piece that requires so much as a tug once you are dressed or that makes you feel like you can't breathe comfortably is a piece to skip. From experience on the set, from feedback about comfort, breathability, and the all-important "I didn't feel it or think about it once it was on my body" factor, I've worked out the **fit details** on the following pieces.

Body Suits

- **The Body Wrap line**—The *ne plus ultra* of body shapers, seamless, molding, and deceptively lightweight with firm control, underwire bra cups.
- **Wacoal**—Seamless control body suit in cups up to DD
- **Bali**—Body by Bali Concealers—Seamless, convertible bra straps
- **Flexees**—Controlwear
- **TC**—Seamless, underwire bodysuit

Lower Body Shapers

- **Spanx**—Power pants for lightweight control-top smoothing from waist to below knee
- **Victoria's Secret**—Footless Control Top
- **Nancy Ganz**—Wonderwear, Capri Length Panty (in light and medium control)
- **Nancy Ganz**—What a Waist, Capri Length with a waist shaper
- **Underwonder**—Various pants for tummy, tummy and hips, tummy to thighs
- **Underwonder**—Waistshapers (styled like bike shorts, to midthigh)
- **Hanes**—Body Enhancers
- **Bali**—Body by Bali briefs and thigh slimmers

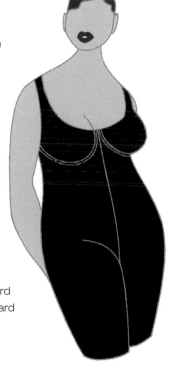

Allover

This stylist's number one pick for flawless, line-free shaping: the unitard. In my experience with voluptuous singers and actresses (also actresses postpregnancy) lightweight unitards are a line-free solution that moves with the body.

- **Body Wrap**—Seamless, firm control unitard
- **Nancy Ganz**—Firm Control Unitard
- **Nancy Ganz**—Bodyshaping Unitard

Bra Slips

- **Body Wrap**—Bra slip
- **Flexees**—Body slip that doesn't ride up when you walk
- **Lane Bryant**—Cacique Body Slip

more illusions

▶ **Breast pads:** Known as *chicken cutlets*, they come in different cup sizes; for the most natural look choose your actual size in full shapes that cover the entire breast. Demishapes add a bump from the side or from the base of the bra. They also come in different materials—the somewhat weighty silicone, and the water and air styles that have a nylon exterior. Again, every girl's shape is slightly different so experiment a bit with the bra(s) you wear most. Remember, the most important trick with enhancers is to go for *a subtle, natural* lift and enhancement rather than a volcanic eruption.

▶ **Strapless/backless:** Fashion Forms Divine Body-Bra: a pair of silicone "cutlets" joined together at the breastbone by a plastic clip. Treated with an adhesive that reacts with your skin, the inside of the pads stick to your breasts, no straps required. They don't budge, they don't show, and they are a solution for added cleavage for strapless and backless looks (for cups A, B, and C).

▶ **Nippits:** Painless adhesive tapes that conceal your nipples for bra-less or under sheer bras. Even if you are among the camp that loves the look of erect nipples in a T-shirt, keep in mind that they become an all too obvious focal point. Wouldn't you rather have guys looking at your face as you walk down the street? Order online from **nippits.com**.

▶ **Bra extenders:** If you fall into a half size between two band measurements use a bra extender. Lingerie stores will sew them on for you or order online from **fashionforms.com**.

▶ **Shoulder pads:** For type A and type D girls—dolman shoulder pads with a line that extends over the natural shoulder have the most natural, least detectable look under cotton tees, silk shirts. Department stores or **fashionforms.com** and **kathleenkirkwood.com**.

▶ **Toupee tape:** Reincarnated as Hollywood Fashion Tape. As I mentioned earlier, toupee tape is one way a stylist makes a stubborn piece of fabric lie flat against the skin or adheres one piece of fabric to another. But a real woman trying to negotiate an evening out in a plunging neckline with nothing between her and public exposure but a piece of tape is a recipe for disaster. On the set, as a model moves, the stylist must constantly adjust the tape as it catches on the fabric. Just because you've read in *Us Weekly* that your favorite actress negotiated a press line in a plunging neckline held together with a little tape, bear in mind that she also had to maintain an excruciatingly erect posture to pull off her photo ops and keep that neckline in place. Talk to her about tape after she'd had a few cocktails and tried to dance. Tape can be a great quick fix for gapping at the bustline in a button-front or wrap-front shirt or for an emergency hem at the office. Find it at beauty supply stores, lingerie stores.

▶ **Bustiers/corsets:** One last tip from Rebecca Apsan at La Petite Coquette. Since the store does a brisk business in corsets that are worn as evening wear, I asked her for a few particulars on fit: "When you put on a corset you should feel taller, more erect, and your breasts pushed up. The hem of the corset should clear the waistband of your bottom for a smooth, gap-free line. If the circumference of the corset puts you into a cup that is slightly big for you, it's very easy to add a bump pad from the bottom for the needed pushup effect. If you are spilling out of the top or side of the cups, keep looking."

HAVING SORTED OUT YOUR wardrobe and foundations, it's time to send you on to the beauty experts. Hair and makeup stars have as keen an eye for line, proportion, and color as the best fashion stylists, so it is a given that they will be a part of your fitting. They will have reviewed the final outfit choices with me—head to toe—to carefully consider the right look and feeling for you and for what you will be wearing. Next stop, the hairstylist's chair.

hair

Nothing is more critical to the overall success of a picture (or your look walking down the street, for that matter) than the right haircut. In a photograph, the fashion styling may be flawless, the makeup luminous but, if the hairdresser has missed the mark, there is no salvaging the picture. It's the same for all of us in real life. You may be someone who arrives at an uncomplicated style and stays with it for years, like a bob that never really dates, as it can be easily tweaked every season with the addition of lengths, a long bang, a razored edge, or a precision line to keep the look current. Or you might be the woman who embraces a new runway look just as fast as your hair can grow out of the last big look. Whatever your style, pay attention to your hair and embrace change, subtle or otherwise. Your approach to your hair and your approach to your wardrobe should be in step with one another. Reevaluate one and make sure that you reevaluate the other.

I've asked **Kevin Mancuso**, hairstylist to celebrities like Salma Hayek, Britney Spears, Jennifer Connelly, Julianna Margulies, Cindy Crawford, and Molly Sims, among others, the author of *The Mane Thing* (Little Brown) and *Allure* contributor to share his tips for getting a great haircut.

▶ **Talk about it:** Kevin advises that the best way to communicate with your hairstylist is to plan ahead. Think of it sort of as an interview. Make a wish list and a *don't wish* list. Narrow things down so you can clearly communicate what you want. You must understand the texture of your hair, and whether it will allow you to achieve the style you want. Choose a hairstylist based on a recommendation from someone whose haircut you liked (preferably someone with a similar texture to your own). Collect some magazine pictures and show them to your stylist to communicate the look you hope to achieve.

When you get to the salon be sure that the stylist sees you with *dry* hair (as you walk in) and takes the time to speak with you. Be open to your stylist's suggestions. Let the stylist speak first, so he or she can tell you what they visualize working best for the shape of your face and the texture of your hair.

▶ **Proportion and texture:** Kevin says, "The first thing I do is look at the person from head to toe: her body type, the shape of her face, and what she is wearing. I try to get a sense of her lifestyle. What does she do in a day, how much time does she have to spend on hair maintenance, what kind of versatility does she need from her cut? I feel her hair's natural texture to assess what kind of texture I can cut into it and ultimately what will suit her best."

▶ **Color:** Color is a natural complement to a new haircut since it is a great way of creating movement in hair and a more three-dimensional look for the cut and style. The use of color around the hairline is an ideal way to lighten and open up a face; it is also an effective contouring frame. Color communicates your personality (sophisticated, whimsical, bad ass, hard, soft) so talk with your stylist about how adding some color can enhance the look you begin with your haircut. Color also changes and enhances hair texture and can add greater pliability for ease in styling; it adds needed volume to fine hair and can soften coarse hair that is hard to style and to straighten.

▶ **The biggest mistakes:** "Don't try to imitate celebrities and models. Chances are their hair texture is very different from yours—not to mention that a stylist has probably spent considerable time to achieve the look you see in the picture—whether in a fashion story or on the red carpet." Again, let your stylist give you an honest evaluation of what you want based on your hair's texture, the shape of your face, and your overall body type.

▶ **Be realistic:** "Another critical mistake that women make is not being realistic about the time required to maintain a style. They may keep up with it for a week and then the time required seems like too much and they are ultimately disappointed with the results." Talk honestly with your stylist. He or she can help you understand the versatility and limitations of your hair and your ability to achieve any style.

makeup:
tips from the pros

Aside from working with incredible clothes and accessories, one of the things I enjoy most about my job is watching talented makeup artists work their magic on the canvas of a clean face. I've learned from the very best in the business that it takes very little makeup to enhance a face, to create an even-toned complexion, to accentuate eyes and lips. The best makeup artists use only what is essential to create those glowing, so-called natural faces we all fall in love with on the beauty pages.

Compare those modern images of beauty to the look of the typical saleswoman behind a cosmetics counter in a department store. One word always comes to mind: *caked*. Lots of makeup, lots of color, shadowing, contouring, lining, and powdering. An ideal look for a regional production of *The Mikado* perhaps, but not a look for any woman with style.

Aside from creating distinctive, natural faces on models, one of the most striking similarities among female makeup artists is that they wear very little makeup—if any—themselves. What makeup they do wear is blended for the sheerest effect to accentuate clean, clear, moist skin enhanced by subtle, tonal color. Want to look older? No, I didn't think so. Think back to when, as a teenager, you wanted to pass yourself as more grownup to get into a club. Uh-huh, me too. I piled on the makeup. When a very young model turns up for a shoot and the client decides she needs to look older, the makeup artist will create a strong, heavily lined or shadowed eye, the lips will become defined and darker. The plain truth? More makeup is not more of a good thing; rather, it is instantly aging.

Since the illusory power of makeup is considerable, it makes good sense to perfect an everyday face (that you can do in ten minutes or less) that is natural, healthy-looking, and allows your skin to show through any products you apply. Trendproof, ageproof, timeless style. Any heavy artillery at the dermatologist or plastic surgeon aside, get this part of your routine perfected and you will always be the woman whose age is hard to pin down.

If you've ever been confounded by formulations when choosing skin care or by the right tonal matches when testing concealers and foundations, join a vast sorority of women. Here's what **Bobbi Brown**, beauty expert and founder of Bobbi Brown Professional Cosmetics, advises:

"As a makeup artist, I've always believed that any great look begins with the basics: skin care, concealer, foundation, and powder. Get these makeup essentials right, and you'll always look like you have naturally perfect skin. Know your skin. Diet, weather, and stress can affect skin on a daily basis, so it's important to have different skin-care options instead of blindly reaching for the same products every day."

Skin care

▶ **Cleanser:** "If you have a dry complexion, use a cream cleanser that moisturizes as it cleanses. Look for ingredients like wheat germ oil, which cleans without stripping, and glycerin, which attracts moisture to the skin's surface. Water-based gel cleansers with oil-fighting ingredients like seaweed extract are perfect for oily complexions. Ideally, you should have two cleansers—one for days when skin is a bit oilier than normal or needs extra cleaning, and another for days when skin feels a bit drier. Never use body soap on your face; it will strip skin, leaving it feeling tight and dry."

▶ **Moisturizer:** "This is the most important step in caring for skin. When skin isn't well moisturized, it looks dull, tired, and older than it really is. Try a lightweight moisturizing lotion if you have normal skin. Opt for a richer, hydrating cream with ingredients like petrolatum, glycerin, or shea butter when skin feels dry or sensitive. And, contrary to popular belief, even oily skin benefits from moisturizer. Try an oil-free formula that hydrates while it helps control overactive oil production."

▶ **Sunscreen:** "You should wear sun protection factor (SPF) year round, not just in the summer. A lotion with an SPF of 15 to 30 is key whenever you're outdoors. Apply sunscreen before moisturizer and makeup. A moisturizer with sunscreen is just as effective for daily use."

▶ **Eye cream:** "The skin around the eyes is more delicate than the rest of your face and has special needs. Use eye cream morning—before applying concealer—and night."

Bobbi Brown adds, "After cleansing and moisturizing, take a moment to look at yourself in the mirror to figure out how much makeup you actually need. There will be days when you only need concealer to feel better, and other days when you need the more polished look of foundation and powder."

Concealer

"This is my biggest beauty must. Concealer is designed to cover dark under-eye circles and can instantly make you look well rested. Look for a smooth, creamy formula that's yellow-based and one shade lighter than your skin tone. Use your finger or a concealer brush to apply a generous amount of concealer under the eye up to the lash-line and at the innermost corners. Smooth and blend by gently tapping with the pads of your fingers. If you still see darkness, apply a second layer. To make concealer long lasting, use a powder puff to layer on a dusting of pale yellow powder."

Foundation

"Foundation helps eliminate redness and even out skin tone. Start by finding the formula that meets your skin's needs and your lifestyle." Foundation formulas range from sheer, tinted moisturizers to compact foundations with a lot of coverage. Test foundation by swatching it on the side of your face—not on your hand or arm—and checking your reflection in natural light. The right shade of foundation should seem to disappear into your skin. Use your fingers or a sponge to apply foundation."

Powder

"I finish off with powder to give foundation staying power, take away shine, and give skin a smooth, polished look. Look for a sheer powder with a silky, lighter-than-air texture. Stay away from translucent powders, which can make skin look pasty and ashy. Use a powder puff to apply powder, dusting off excess with a powder brush. Pressed powder compacts are good for on-the-go touchups."

Another tip your stylist has learned behind the scenes from makeup pros: it's smart to use one skin-flattering color on your cheeks, lips, and even eyes. This strategy works in your twenties and will keep working forevermore. Makeup color trends—providing they flatter your individual coloring—are one of the fastest (and relatively inexpensive) ways to move your look along every season, but choosing subtle, current-looking color and applying it with a light hand is the key to a luminous look.

Makeup artist **Sonia Kashuk**, the author of *Real Beauty* (Clarkson Potter) whose makeup and skin-care line is available at Target stores, offers the following advice for choosing and using **color cosmetics**: "I believe that women always look most beautiful in less makeup. Less makeup means more of the woman and her individual spirit shining through."

▸ Think of the colors you choose as a final accessory for your overall look. Use your hair color and the clothing colors that flatter you best as a guide when you shop for makeup.

▸ Always look at colors in natural light. If a color looks appealing and natural in sunlight, then you are safe in any light. Do your makeup in natural light for this reason as well. You will tend to use

less. For the most natural-looking results, any color products you choose should go on with a sheer finish to allow your skin to show through the color.

▶ Blush colors should always look as real as possible. Think of the color your cheeks naturally flush when you blush or exercise. Colors that flatter your specific skin tone—colors like rose and mauve for skin with blue/red skin tones and peach and coral tones for yellow/brown skin tones—are classic complements. Always apply blush to the apple of your cheek. When using a cream formulation, blend it very lightly with your fingers. You can always add a bit more color to achieve the desired brightness. For powder blushes, it is essential to apply blush lightly with a blush brush for sheer, even results.

▶ Stay with the same tone for the color you wear on your lips. To create a fuller-looking lip, use a lip brush. If you use a lip liner, moisten your lips lightly first with lip balm then fill in the entire lip with liner and apply a sheer application of lipstick on top. Be sure to keep the edges blended and soft.

▶ The most natural-looking way to define your eyes is to add a little emphasis at the base of your lash line with shadow in colors like chocolate, charcoal, even navy, to keep the line from looking too harsh. Using a smudge brush, which has a small, fine tip; blend it gently. Using soft colors like taupe or beige, brush a small amount of shadow in the crease of your lid to create contour and depth for your eye. Curl your lashes to open up your eyes, and apply a coat of mascara to your upper lashes.

▶ Brows should be filled in with a sharpened brow pencil or a powder and brow brush. Choose a color as close to your brow color as possible and fill in lightly between hairs only where needed with short, light strokes.

▶ To create balance and symmetry for your face, avoid the clash of too many colors. If your brows are heavily penciled, along with strong use of color at your eyes and again at your cheeks and lips, you detract from rather than complement your natural features. When you use strong color to emphasize one area, for example, a strong red or berry mouth, keep the rest of your face neutral and go very light on the blush. If you emphasize your eyes with a smoky shadow for evening, wear a soft, pale lipstick.

> No makeup bag should be without an eyelash curler, a lip brush, a powder/blush brush, a smudge brush for eye lining, and a larger brush for applying shadow on the lids, a Spoolie or lash comb for brows, and a good pair of tweezers.

eyebrows and nails

Your **eyebrows** are an essential focal point for your face. Your **hands** are another visible and highly expressive focal point. It's a critical part of your grooming to pay close attention to their upkeep. Both of these elements are considered a big enough deal in pictures that, in order to assure that a model's brows have just the right shape for her eyes and the shape of her face, a brow specialist is often a part of the beauty team on cosmetics advertising shoots. And her hands are massaged and manicured to complement the rest

Dida Paraschivoiu is an aesthetician who specializes in eyebrows and manicures and is often the expert who attends to these finishing details on the set. Girls on both sides of the camera beg for her precision brow shapings and luxury manicures. Some advice from Dida:

Eyebrows

"It's always best to have your eyebrows professionally shaped. Just as you probably wouldn't be able to cut your own hair and achieve a professional-looking line, to achieve a perfectly balanced frame for your face, go to someone who is trained to draw the line with their tweezers and scissors. A professional will trim the tops of your brow with small scissors to create a more precise symmetry. Don't try cutting your brows at home. Once the right shape is reached, ask for instructions that will help you best maintain the line between appointments.

"Never wax your brows! The muscles under the brow are thin and the skin over them is delicate. Over time, waxing stretches this very delicate skin.

Here are Dida's tips for achieving the right frame for your face:

> Buy good quality tweezers (she uses Tweezerman). Use one pair with a pointed tip for drawing and a pair with a slanted tip for cleaning. Pluck your eyebrows during the day in natural light; ideally, set

up a mirror in front of a window. *Always take your time.* With the slant-tip tweezers, clean the area between your brows. Trace a line up from the inner corner of your eye. This is the beginning of your brow. Be careful not to remove any hairs from this area.

▶ Next, clean the area below your brow, which will begin to open up your eye. Pluck only the hairs under your brow. The shape of your eyebrow should mirror the shape of your cheekbone. Look at the shape of your cheekbone—trace it with your hand—and visualize the cheekbone as the bottom half of a circle with the top half being your brow.

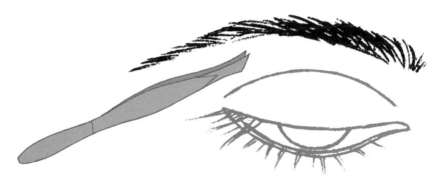

▶ From the inner corner of your eye, trace a straight line upward to your brow. With the pointed tip, pluck one hair at a time, step back, look in the mirror. Go easy, continuing one hair at a time, as this is a gradual incline.

▶ When you reach the point at which you can trace a straight line up from the outer edge of your iris, this is the beginning of your arch. Pluck a few more hairs at a time until you can trace a straight line upwards from the outer corner of your eye. This is where the arch ends and where the line of your brow should start to move downward. The end of your brow should reach beyond the outer corner of your eye.

▶ Never tweeze the top of your brows.

If you've overplucked and want to grow out your brow line, lightly pencil in a thicker line using a pencil in a shade as close to your natural color as possible. Pluck only those hairs that don't conform to the new shape until your brows have grown out.

Manicure

Dida says: "I can tell everything about a woman by her nails. If she bites her nails and picks at her cuticles, her emotional life is generally a wreck. If she wears long nails and colorful polish, she has a pretty leisurely life, as to keep up a look like this you can't use your hands much."

The ideal (and most chic) length for nails is just covering the tips of your fingers. The nails must all be one length, and what always looks clean and modern is a sheer, nude polish. It extends the finger line and makes the hands look very graceful. Have your nails done, or keep up with them yourself, once a week.

Dida's recipe for the perfect manicure at home

- Remove any polish with nonacetone remover
- File your nails to one length. The shape of your nail should follow the natural shape of the *moon*, or white of your nail, at the base.
- Soak your cuticles well, then gently push them back with an orange-wood stick wrapped in a little cotton and soaked in vitamin E oil. *Never cut your cuticles.* Gently buff away any dead rough skin with a buffing block. If you have any hangnails, this is the time to use cuticle scissors and nip them away.
- Cream your hands well. Always apply cream to moist hands—it will absorb better into your skin.
- Wipe your hands of excess cream with a warm, wet washcloth and remove any residue of cream and oil from your nails (it prevents the polish from adhering) with a cotton ball and nail-polish remover.
- Apply base coat, then paint your color polish in three strokes; one up the center and one on each side; apply top coat. Allow a few minutes between coats for the best results.

Now a last word on manicures and pedicures from your stylist, as they relate to your clothes. I have never met a woman with great personal style who wears her fingernails long, or long and bright, or long, pale and frosty, painted with tiny designs, or adorned with rhinestones. When nails are this prominent, they become another accessory in your outfit rather than a subtle finish, and the effect plays like cheap plastic bangles. Bright clothing with bright nails? Too much. Chipped dark nail polish? Works for girls who play bass guitar by night and sleep by day—unkempt and just plain grubby for the rest of us. Aim for nails groomed to perfection and just covering the fingertip with a dark polish—for a cool sophistication.

Now, your **feet**. Summertime sandals mean a pedicure every few weeks. Dirty feet, callused heels, chipped toenail polish—well, come on. Ladies, carry baby wipes with you. If you trek scalding city streets in sandals like your stylist, give your feet a wipe during the day just as you wash your hands. Especially if you wear a light colored toenail polish, pale colors get scuffed and dirty-looking. Give 'em a little buff with a towelette.

Nail goddess Dida P. weighs in once again with her recipe for an easy pedicure at home.

▶ Remove any polish with nonacetone remover.

▶ Using a clipper specifically for toenails (Tweezerman makes a good one), clip your nails straight across. Be careful not to cut below the tips of your toes and do not clip the sides. File nails into a square/oval—a slightly rounded square shape.

▶ Apply cuticle cream to your cuticles.

▶ While this works, gently buff the dry soles and heels of your feet with a heel file or foot rasp (again, Tweezerman makes a very good one).

▶ Soak your feet for about five minutes in warm water with a little shower gel and a teaspoon of hydrogen peroxide or laundry bleach if your nails are yellowed.

▶ Very gently push your cuticles back with an orangewood stick covered in a little cotton and soaked in vitamin E oil. Rub a damp washcloth over the tops of your toes to remove any calluses or rough skin there or rub your feet with an exfoliating scrub.

- After rinsing your feet thoroughly, cover them in lotion and wrap them in hot, damp hand towels, and rest with your feet elevated for about ten minutes. (This is a nice time to apply cucumber slices to your eyes as well.) Wipe excess cream off your nails with a cotton swab soaked in remover. If you don't have a pair of rubber toe separators, wind a piece of tissue or rolled paper towel between your toes.

- Apply a base coat or a ridge filler if your nails are not smooth, followed by two coats of polish and a top coat. Again, apply your polish in three strokes, one up the center and one on each side, and if any polish bleeds onto to your cuticles, wipe it away with an orangewood stick dipped in remover.

- Let your toes dry for an hour. Put your feet up and relax.

"THIS IS NO DRESS REHEARSAL, THIS IS LIFE!" a cosmetics saleswoman once barked at me when I declined to add a $250 miracle skin cream to my purchase. While I passed on the cream, she did start me thinking about the unseen preparations that can make or break a woman's look—the *pre-dress* rehearsals, you might say. *What lies beneath* the look of any confident, well-groomed woman is someone who understands the importance of all the elements detailed in this chapter.

Master the foundation elements and the ease with which you can put yourself together every day will be surprisingly routine. And ease is the operative word here. How many of us have plunked down lots of money for miracle shapewear, new cosmetics, or a new haircut, only to have bought into something so high maintenance that we can't possibly make the changes stick in our everyday lives? Your stylist doesn't advocate the kind of glossy perfection that creates an appearance done to the extreme; what we've talked about in this chapter are the essentials, the non-negotiables. What lies beneath your look is central to your everyday style, now and always. ●

7 accessories

Nothing better articulates your sense of style and personality than your choice of accessories. How you accessorize, the bag you carry, the heel on your shoe, the scale of your jewelry all conduct a conversation with the world at large and speak volumes about your sense of individuality. Accessories are the surest way to capture a *fashion moment*. They can also be a serious investment, so it is critical to understand how to buy what complements your silhouette as well as your wardrobe. Spending on good accessories for both day and night is a sensible way to expand the scope of your closet. Nothing elevates those indispensable pieces like a well-considered combination of shoes, bag, and jewelry.

For everyday, it can be a simple as this: a distinctive handbag, a shoe of the season, sunglasses that fit your face perfectly, a clean-lined watch. This essential foursome always pulls a look together. Of course, it is considerably more fun to add a little jewelry, a belt, or throw on a scarf. Knowing how to combine accessories and have them finish rather than compete with your clothes (and each other) is what separates fashion amateurs from girls with great personal style.

shoes, glorious shoes

A classic female obsession, and with good reason. A great pair of shoes elevates everything else in an outfit. Whether you take an archival approach, stockpiling beloved pairs by the dozens, or maintain a pared-down group of current essentials, we love our shoes because they add instant charm, cheek, and sexiness to an outfit. Your shoes are *a very big deal,* as few things in your wardrobe reveal more about your taste level and eye for detail. *Very cheap shoes are very telling*. It's tougher to fake it with cheap shoes than it is with any other inexpensive piece of clothing. Spend on the best pairs you can possibly afford, as it is always better to have a few pairs of great quality than boxes full of cheapies.

High Heels

Never buy high heels that hurt. No matter that a shoe is a hysteria-inducing *masterpiece* in the display case or the designer markdown of the century—if you cannot walk in them for a sustained period of time they are a complete waste of money. The tacit relationship we have with high heels is that we'll put up with some discomfort for a style of beautiful design, for the alchemy of a shoe that magically lengthens the leg by 4 inches, slims the foot, and narrows the ankle. There is no denying the pleasure of slipping one's foot into a gorgeous shoe, but the notion that without pain there is no pleasure is bunk.

Like every other body adornment shoes have certain design features that distinguish the way they will fit. Along with the aesthetic considerations, pay attention to these aspects of **fit** when you try on a pair of heels.

▶ **Last:** All shoe designers create replicas of a woman's foot for each and every style they produce. Either wood or plastic, the *last* establishes the *arch* and, consequently, how well your weight is distributed along the length of your foot. Just like the rise in a pair of pants, if your natural arch doesn't conform well to the last, you'll feel it as you walk in them. Leave them in the box and keep looking.

▶ **Shank:** The curve of the shoe just under the arch. Your body's weight is absorbed at the shank by the ball of your foot and across your instep (top of your foot), as you walk. The strength and quality here will determine how comfortable you feel and how well you can walk.

▶ **Quarter:** The back of the shoe and where it hits your foot. If it is too high it can dig into the side of your ankle, and if it is too low it won't offer the right stability and support.

▶ **Vamp:** How low a shoe is cut toward your toes. Obviously a low vamp will give you a little toe cleavage and a very high vamp may have a foot-, ankle-, and leg-thickening effect.

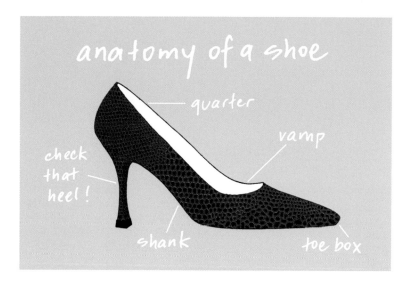

anatomy of a shoe

quarter

vamp

check that heel!

shank

toe box

▶ **Toe box:** Whether the toe is pointed, rounded, square, or open, make sure that the extended line it creates is both comfortable and a flattering one for the length of your leg, your foot, and your overall proportion.

▶ **Heel height:** We all have our limits. Aside from runway models (who are coached to walk in skyscraping heels) women who can actually walk well in a 4-inch stiletto and accommodate the shift in her center of gravity and the slightly forward pitch of her body are in the minority, and have probably had some dance training. Aside from the height of a heel, pay attention to *the turn* of a heel and whether it is an essentially straight line to the ground or if it curves inward toward the arch or outward toward the back of your foot. How these elements come together in the design will separate the shoe you can walk in from one that will have you hobbled by noon. Walkability and aesthetics generally come together with a heel height of 2 to 3½ inches and a sculpted (not needle thin) or sleek stacked heel.

▶ **Heel width:** Another consideration. While the words *sturdy, comfortable,* or *orthodic* may come to mind when you see a pair of feet and legs in a pump or Mary Jane with a low, chunky heel, this will never be a shoe silhouette that elevates your style profile. If you are not comfortable in more than a 1 to 1½ inch heel don't abandon style for comfort. Try a sleek (and easy to walk in) kitten heel to raise your body line a bit and streamline your legs.

When you try on a pair of heels, be sure to look at yourself in a full-length mirror and *take in your entire silhouette*. Do you look and feel balanced? Next, walk in them—not just a quick back and forth. Rather, walk the length of the department or boutique *several times*. Just stand in them as well to get a real sense of your comfort (or lack thereof) and sense of balance in the construction. I never let a salesperson rush me. I walk and stand until I'm sure that the arch and the angle of the heel will suit the contours of my feet and that I feel aligned as I move. A **heel** (at any price) with the wrong shape or height for your silhouette will break up your body line, throw off your best alignment and, frankly, blow your overall look.

Indispensable Shoes

Just as with ready-to-wear, do your research. Walk the shoe departments and pay attention to the seasonal offerings from the designers that generate the most runway buzz. Since many of the shoes (and bags) in a collection that are singled out by the press are certain to be interpreted in a season, you'll spot similar looks all along the fashion food chain. One or two current or trendy shoes can move your whole closet along in a season. More critically, pay attention to the shoe designers whose collections have a *signature* look—whose heels and toes change very little (or not at all) from year to year. These are the trendproof designs you'll want to buy or approximate in your price range for **indispensables** like pumps and a pair of clean-lined boots. Good examples: Manolo Blahnik (as I mentioned earlier, the most imitated heels and toe box in the universe of footwear), Christian Louboutin, Jimmy Choo are all liberally knocked off for distinctive styles based on modern, clean lines, and luxe finishes.

There are certain indispensable shoes that no wardrobe should be without, ever. I always buy updates of these styles for private clients *and* my own wardrobe. The following are the essentials, but if you share your stylist's unrestrained lust for shoes this is only a necessary first step.

▶ **The black pump:** The little black dress *and* crisp white shirt of your shoe wardrobe and just as necessary. Something with a slightly low vamp for a *hint* of toe cleavage so that they are not too racy for a conservative office, but can still have a separate life with the rest of your wardrobe. A classic pointed toe box is sleek-looking and a 2 to 3½ inch heel is ideal for a sexy, high-arched line. These should shout expensive. This is the pair that will elevate those Club Monaco sale skirts or dress up your jeans. Shell it out for the best pair you can afford, then treat them well. Better to resole and frequently touch up the heels on a truly good pair than have several cheap pairs. Cheap black leather seldom looks anything but cheap. Your warm weather variation: the same essential shape in a slingback.

▶ **Tall black boots:** In good leather or stretch leather that give you the same expensive-looking versatility as your black pumps. The line that a boot creates from your foot up your calf is critical to your selection. It should appear to mold to your leg. They shouldn't buckle or look wide at the ankle. Any boot that gaps significantly at the top of your leg is a boot you should bypass.

▶ **Ankle boots:** Combined with a pair of well-cut pants creates an unbroken leg line. Keep the look monochromatic or tonal: black with black or navy; dark espresso brown with dark brown; a rich brown, cordovan, or camel for lighter brown shades; ivory, and white.

▶ **The bad-weather boot:** A regional consideration, of course, for any girl who has ever sacrificed a pair of good boots to wet weather. Find something that suits your life and personality. Whether you choose an urban and chic tall boot in black rubber or patent leather with a flat or low rubber heel, or a cheeky take on the classic Wellington boot, have something in your closet to help you negotiate rain- or snow-soaked streets and spare your good boots.

▶ **The reliable evening shoe:** Most of us shop for evening shoes for specific outfits and events but it is a very good idea to have one closed toe evening shoe in black satin, for example, that is sexy enough to elevate your indispensable black pants or skirt and an evening top or to pair with a tuxedo look. This is the shoe that takes you to any occasion for which a sandal is inappropriate; it will also carry you through an evening out in cold weather when a sandal is obviously the wrong choice. (Whenever I watch girls negotiate an arctic winter evening, bare-legged in stiletto sandals, three words come to mind: *complete fashion victim.* Yes, bare legs and sandals are a combination that fashion loves and that designers promote, because it is clean, modern, and uncomplicated with

classic black pump

two-tone

ballet flats

boot

kitten heel

wild card

d'orsay

sling

clothes. But sometimes a bare foot and leg look ridiculous (for hosiery tips *see* chapter 6).

▶ **Tall evening boot:** Chic in satin and another viable cold weather option. Buy a pair with a classic toe and heel, meaning a pointed toe box and a slim, sculpted 2½ to 3½ inch heel and hang on to them. I'm working on year four with a black satin pair that I treat lovingly and that have seen me through many a winter cocktail party worn with my trusty black pencil skirt and an evening top, a chiffon skirt and a black sweater, or a chiffon slip dress and a shawl.

▶ **Metallic sandals:** It can be very handy to have something simple in leather in a burnished or matte silver, gold, or bronze. Again go for a sleek 2 to 3½ inch heel and a rounded sole at the toe for a look that doesn't date. The spark of a metallic is a definitive *quick-change* element in your wardrobe that elevates the simple indispensable pieces and is perfect with any cocktail dress.

▶ **Old-school trainers:** Comfort and style do not have to be mutually exclusive. I am begging you to stow those chunky workout sneakers in your gym bag and buy a pair of something flat, low, and old-school simple to wear with jeans. Many old school styles are a bargain. It's a veritable sneaker universe out there, so finding a comfortable pair with a little dash is a snap.

▶ **Flat thong sandals:** Whether you are navigating the sands of a beach resort or a scorching urban pavement have at least one pair as unadorned and uncomplicated as your favorite pair in rubber, but in leather or suede, in a color; a neutral; a matte metallic. The "refined" flip-flop raises the bar for warm weather prints, won't add any complication to an outfit worn with distinctive jewelry, and adds a note of sophistication to the basic uniform of a jeans skirt and ribbed cotton tank.

TIP: Synonymous with sandal—*pedicure.* Girls, I've seen the worst walking violations on the streets of New York City among legions of flip-flop shod feet that look, well, *really filthy!* It's a simple connection to make; when you display your feet as prominently as sandwiches on a plate, be sure that they look clean, your heels are buffed, and that your toenails are well groomed. If you think people aren't looking at your feet, *think again.*

Shoe Caveats

Short/ petite girls: Two to three inch heels are an ideal and lengthening proportion. In higher heels, petites often appear pitched forward, their center of gravity thrown off as they walk.

Very curvy girls: Watch out for very high, needle-thin heels. Opt for 2 to 3½ inches and a sleek, sculpted or stacked heel for a more proportionate look.

Full calves and ankles: A woman is usually her own best judge of any shoe that makes her calves and ankles appear thick and yet I see girls every day in ankle straps, ankle ties, and ankle-high boots *with skirts* that make their calves and ankles look much larger than they are. On the set, we call it the "cankle" effect and yes, it happens to models too. Any detail at your ankle will break up the line of your leg *and* always have a thickening effect. Unless your legs are long and thin, opt for a low vamp pump or mule, a d'Orsay pump, and knee-high boots in leather (or leather with stretch) with your skirts. If you love the look but it doesn't flatter you, wear ankle straps and T-straps with your jeans or indispensable pants.

All girls: Unless you play guitar in a KISS tribute band, run from very chunky, black rubber platform bottoms on any shoe. The line is as sexy as wearing two blocks of concrete on your feet. Not to mention that they don't do much for a girl's legs. Very short girls end up looking potted. Try a streamlined wedge heel instead.

Double Agents

This go-anywhere quality is just as useful in your choice of accessories as it is in clothing.

▶ **Two-toned:** Look for modern riffs on the classic two-toned spectator or multi-toned combinations of leather, patent leather, and suede in a pump, d'Orsay, or T-strap. This is a very style- and value-conscious way to pull a shoe into your wardrobe that will spark the look of just about anything in your closet from jeans to a suit.

▶ **Sport shapes:** Like old-school trainers, Birkenstock sandals (a classic style like the Boston) reinterpreted in unexpected fabrics like brocade, corduroy, wool felt, metallic patent leathers, lizard. Comfortable when you must be built for speed and a chic mix with flat-front trousers, trouser-cut denims.

▶ **Flats:** With the girly charm (and comfort) of a nod to the ballet slipper. Look for a low vamp and a flexible hard bottom, so that they bend with your foot, in colored calfskin, patent, or metallic leather, in fabrics like brocade, satin, canvas. From designer offerings to authentic slippers from India, Morocco, or China, these are the solution to finding a flat shoe that adds a distinct, cool elegance to any casual look.

▶ **Wild card:** Pumps or sandals in a statement (trend) color that add a right-now element to anything you wear them with. These are meant to boost those neutral indispensables—the khakis, blacks, whites, last year's black-and-white polka-dot skirt. These are fun, seasonal, and while they don't need to cost a fortune, they also shouldn't be (or look) very cheap, as cheap brights and fabrics seldom look anything but cheap. Bright-colored leather should be the best quality you can afford. Treat these as you would a neutral shoe and wear them a lot in the season. Other suggestions: animal prints, brocades, and silk prints.

Bargain Shoes

Trendy, momentary looks are often the best things to buy *interpreted*, at a bargain if you are on a tight budget. Know your references and run through this checklist to find the most convincing styles that look well made.

▶ **Overall finish:** Run your hands over the leather to feel the smoothness and to make sure that there are no seams that will wrinkle or buckle with wear.

▶ **Material:** Look for matte finishes. Cheap cowhide with a shiny, plasticlike finish screams cheap. Bargain suede can look as rough as sandpaper. If the leather or suede is cardboard stiff, pass. Check the edge of any suede where it meets your foot. It should have a smooth finish with no ragged edges.

▶ **Color:** Neutrals like espresso, chocolate, dark camel, metallics, or muted colors that have low-luster finishes (unless they are patent leather, of course). Somehow, the finishes on black and navy are the hardest to fake, even when the styling and hardware pass inspection. For neutral colors, the rim of the sole and heel looks best when they are matched and neutral as well.

▶ **Toes and Heels:** a cheap toe box can look too heavy and badly molded where it meets the sole; cheap heels are often too thick, clunky, or just don't look current enough. Again, study the look of the most expensive shoes, as they will always have sculpted, smooth toe lines and well-proportioned heels. Paying attention to the details at the top will help you spot the very best copies of a look for less money.

▶ **Trims:** stitching should be straight; buckles and any hardware look more expensive when they are burnished or gunmetal, rather than bright yellow gold or white silver.

Do Your Homework

Here are the lines I always buy (budget permitting) or have a close look at to clock the details and reference at lower prices for *Indispensables* and *Double Agents* alike.

Designer/Bridge

Along with the usual designer suspects—*Chanel, Prada, Gucci, Louis Vuitton, YSL Rive Gauche, Christian Dior, Dolce & Gabbana, Balenciaga,* and *Marc Jacobs*—I buy or research the look of:

Manolo Blahnik	Bottega Veneta
Narciso Rodriguez	Tod's
Christian Louboutin	Hogan
Pierre Hardy	Edmundo Castillo
Michel Perry	Donna Karan
Alain Tondowski	Calvin Klein
Alexandra Neel	Michael Kors
Helmut Lang	Vera Wang
Jil Sander	Ralph Lauren
Anya Hindmarch	Sigerson Morrison

Midprice lines

Marc by Marc Jacobs	Furla
Kors, Michael Kors	Coach

Cole Haan	DKNY
Kaki Daniels	Anne Klein
L'Autre Chose	Isaac, Isaac Mizrahi
Hollywould	Delman
Kate Spade	Ellen Tracy

Better Market/Good Buys (and convincing interpretations):

Nine West: Their own boutiques for the fullest selection, better offerings, and improved heels every season.

Via Spiga: Their own boutiques for the fullest selection of new looks.

Unisa: Their own boutiques for the fullest selection of looks inspired by all the biggies, particularly strong for sandals, evening.

BCBG Max Azria: Trendy

Lauren, Ralph Lauren: For boots in particular.

Victoria's Secret catalogue: Their Colin Stuart brand for some of the best, inexpensive designer knockoffs out there, but stick with metallics, neutral browns, and light colors.

Harley-Davidson boots: Real deal boots that consistently inspire designer copies.

Jildor-designer-shoes.com: Designers at discount, but the selection can be limited.

Designershoes.com: Hard-to-find large sizes and wide widths.

Garnethill.com: Often includes chic and witty bad weather boots by Tamara Henriques and Mosquito in their shoe selection.

Flipfloptrunkshow.com: Simple thong sandals and then some.

Sneakers/Trainers

Chuck Taylors: Look good with just about anything casual

Converse One Stars

Stan Smiths

Jack Purcells

Adidas: Italias, sambas, gazelles

Royal Elastic: Groovy slip-ons (they run big and wide, however).

Marc by Marc Jacobs: Does old-school style one better.

Le Coq Sportif

Y3 by Adidas

Eastbay.com: A great source for old-school styles, often at discount.

Trade Secrets
from New York City's best shoe repair service

Well-heeled women all over Manhattan hoof it to midtown's Shoe Service Plus where the staff of footwear artisans performs miracles every day. Here's what proprietor David Mesquita advises for some common shoe dilemmas:

Slingbacks that slip: You know the drill. You wear them once or twice then they slip from your heel. A quick solution, says David, is to have a cobbler insert a half-pad *under* the inner sole liner. This will push the front of your foot backward slightly to close the gap between heel and strap. Failing this measure, a cobbler can take in the strap by removing it from the last and cutting away a tiny amount of strap before reattaching it for a snug fit.

Tall boot too tight at the calves: According to David, "Stretching boots through the calves works best with soft calfskin, as it gives more easily. The boot is placed on a machine that stretches the leather very slowly, with heat, over the course of several hours. Depending on the give in the leather, a boot can be stretched up to two inches of additional give through the calf. The more you stretch a skin, however, the more likely it will be damaged, leaving the leather ridged."

Tall boot too loose at the calves: The side zipper is removed and the width is reduced from the inside of the boot at the back seam, the lining is also narrowed accordingly, and the zipper, is reattached. David says: "we don't recommend taking in a boot at the zipper, as it next to impossible to create a completely even line."

Tall boot too tall for the length of your leg: "A boot can be cut down from the top. The zipper is removed, the excess height is trimmed while maintaining the correct line for the boot—the outer edge of a boot is a quarter inch higher than the inner edge—and the zipper is reattached," adds David.

MAINTENANCE TIPS

- When you buy a new, prize pair take them to the cobbler *before* you wear them. Have a leather tap or plastic tap (depending on the material of the sole) placed at the tip of the toe to prevent scuffing and wear.

- Always keep up with your heels. Don't wait until the leather looks as though it's been worked over with a cheese grater, or the heel tip starts to wear, to have them spruced up.

- Keep them polished between wearing to keep the leather clean and supple. Buy shoe polish and a waterproofing spray and use them. Shoe Service recommends spraying your clean shoes, boots, and handbags with Meltonian Water & Stain Protector as insurance against the elements.

my handbag, myself

I admit it freely. I am a *bagaholic*. I have a fetishistic relationship with my handbags (traceable to age three, when I started carrying one of my mom's satin evening bags with me everywhere). Here's why: *a woman is her handbag*. Different bags reflect different facets of her personality. The bag she carries broadcasts her story to the world or, more to the point, the story she wants to tell, while the contents hold her very private survival kit and intimate secrets.

Carrying a different bag for every day of the week is a sure way to indulge your inner fashion schizophrenic and carrying **the bag of the moment** bestows a kind of seasonal luster to anything you wear. But the one bag that every woman really needs in her wardrobe is a classic to ground the look of anything she wears. A classic bag conveys the cool confidence of carrying something enduring rather than a momentary thing. Particularly if your style is eclectic, a clean-lined shape works with everything. Buy a bag with the **lines**, the **proportion**, and the **materials** (or the best approximation of the materials you can possibly afford) that has been inspired by one of these styles in the following **standard of iconic handbags:**

- Hermès Birkin
- Hermès Plume
- Hermès Bolide
- Hermès Le Trim
- Hermès Kelly
- Louis Vuitton Noe
- Louis Vuitton Speedy
- Chanel 2/1955
- Gucci's cane-handled styles
- Anything tote-inspired by canvas classics like L.L. Bean's Boat and Tote Bag

Many of these styles from the houses of Hermès and Louis Vuitton evolved from turn of the century bags created for travel and purposes like carrying horse blankets, feed, and mail. Top handled styles, created specifically as ladies' bags for travel, inform much of what we covet today. These shapes endure for their ingenious practicality married with elegance and luxury and inspire scores of interpretations every season. While most of us can only dream about owning a spanking new Birkin, for example, as you take a close look at handbags at all prices, you'll notice that many new styles have *referenced* their shapes or hardware in some way from the clean styling of these iconic designs. Play the reference spotting game with these *neoclassic* handbags as you do with ready-to-wear and you will find something with a lasting look that you can afford.

Here are designers whose collections I always look through for chic lines minus a price tag requiring a bank loan.

Neoclassics

Designer

Lambertson Truex: Non-logoed and luxe.

Marc Jacobs: Especially timeless: the Sophia bag.

Prada: Doctor's bag and lunchbox shapes endure.

Fendi: Doctor's bag in the Selleria series is especially timeless and luxe.

Gucci: If you bypass the bag of the minute and any smattering of logos, you'll find simple shapes, wonderful leathers, and those bamboo handles always look right.

Tod's: Classic series of shapes each season.

Hogan: Sports references, luxe materials, and finishes.

Anya Hindmarch: Unique details, beautiful leathers, great shapes.

Bally: Reinvigorated by new designs, same traditional quality.

Bridge/Midprice

Rafe: Among the most luxe midpriced bags out there, great finishes, great hardware.

Sigerson Morrison: Distinctive, original takes on classic shapes, great details and hardware.

Ursule Beaugeste: Very French, very chic pebble-grain leathers with tough hardware.

Vanessa Bruno: Buttery leather totes.

Marc by Marc Jacobs: Clean, no fuss, leather totes.

Barney's Private Label: Great quality classic bags with witty details.

DKNY: Good leathers, colors, details.

Kate Spade: Her strong colors and simple details are distinctive and work as neutrals.

Dooney and Bourke: Tassel is their standout bag, especially in colors.

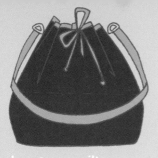

louis vuitton noe

chanel 2/1955

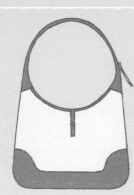

hermes le trim

hermes kelly

hermes plume

louis vuitton speedy

hermes birkin

hermes bolide

Cole Haan: Clean modern designs, great details, expensive looking embossed leathers.

Furla: A range of *iconic* inspirations every season.

Coach: Look for styles revived from the 60s designs for Coach by the late designer Bonnie Cashin for affordable, stand-out classics.

> **TIP:** If you hunger for an authentic icon, log onto Web sites like luxuryvintage.com or eBay, try designer resale shops and vintage and antique stores, and, with luck, discover an original for less. *Less* however is a relative term here. Many highly coveted originals like the Hermès Birkin still cost several thousand dollars online.

> **Color:** Along with construction inspired by an icon, good materials, and clean design, consider investing in a distinctive color rather than limiting your options to black, brown, or saddle. Standouts in hues of red, orange, mid-tone sky blue, kelly green, marigold, mustard, cream, or white. All of these colors function as neutrals and the pop of a rich color with any outfit conveys confidence and style intelligence.

Totes

If good leather is too expensive, consider investing in quality nylon or canvas bag or tote with leather trim, or PVC (rubber) embossed to look like pebble-grain calf. For example:

Vanessa Bruno: Canvas with leather trims and grommets, chic and a little tough.

Un Apres-Midi de Chien: Chic satchels.

Jack Gomme: Canvas with PVC trims.

MZ Wallace: Classic shapes; great details, colors, and materials.

Longchamp: Classic nylons.

Le Sportsac: In solid colors, metallics.

Flight001.com: Luxe-looking PVC travel bags that cross over for work bags.

RO: Chic PVC faux pebble grain calf designed for carry-ons in handbag appropriate sizes.

Brontibay: Snappy and colorful canvas with contrast trim.

Karine DuPont: Cheeky nylon shoulder bags with separate zipped compartments attached to the outside of the bag.

Louison: Witty takes in canvas and nylon on "It" bags.

Kate Spade: Hey, she's built an empire on her totes.

Club Monaco	bagshop.com
Banana Republic	net-a-porter.com
Cole Haan	bluefly.com

And a Few More Ideas

With your classics in place, here are a few more suggestions for your handbag arsenal.

▶ **Weekend, one million errands bag:** Leather, nylon, canvas, or cloth and large enough to hold your wallet, sunglasses, a few small purchases, and, yes, a side pocket for the errands list doesn't hurt. This will also take the pressure off your expensive classic. Don't beat a good investment bag into the ground. Give her a little rest now and then.

▶ **Wild card:** Yep, you need a bag that makes a statement as well. Have fun with colors, textures, pattern, embroidery, beading. This is the bag that can express the side of your personality you don't wear to work. Whether exotic or a little bit retro and girly, wear this one on your wrist or tucked under your arm at a cocktail party, out to dinner, or whenever you need to spark a simple outfit that works day into evening.

▶ **Reliable evening bag:** A slim and elegant envelope, a bracelet bag, or a square top handle style in satin or silk; in black, a rich jewel tone, muted silver or gold to accent black. This is the bag that complements but never competes with a serious evening look.

Have a look at these lines or Web sites for evening bags and wild cards.

Wild Cards

Jamin Puech: Unique shapes and details, pricey.

Isabella Fiore: Witty embroideries and details, great shapes.

Christiana Lapetina-Johnson: Retro beading, silky tassels, references from the twenties and thirties.

Nanette Lepore: Whimsical prints.

Anthropologie stores: Always include detailed and unique bags in the mix of merchandise.

Urban Outfitters	neimanmarcusonline.com
BCBG	blueplatefashion.com
bagshop.com	eziba.com

Reliable Evening Bags

When you invest in a bag with a lasting and quiet appeal, go for very little detail and the best quality you can afford. When the price is too steep, emulate the look and simplicity of the designers here:

Designer

Chanel	Manolo Blahnik
Prada	Calvin Klein
Christian Louboutin	Donna Karan

Midprice

Stuart Weitzman	Banana Republic
Coach	Nine West
Via Spiga	Furla
Unisa	eveningbags.com
DKNY	bagshop.com
Ann Taylor	

Bargain Bags

Again, know those references and you'll find all kinds of bags at a price you can afford. Just as with bargain shoes, pay close attention to the finishes:

▶ **The materials:** Choose what looks the most substantial and what feels supple. Very thin leather, particularly with a plastic sheen, will look cheap. Pebble-grain or embossed textures often look more expensive than smooth surfaces. Wimpy suede with a very rough finish won't fool anyone.

▶ **Topstitching:** Should be straight and uniform.

▶ **Edges:** Leather and suede should be smooth, not raw and ragged.

▶ **Zippers and buckles:** Look for low luster trims, meaning brass coloration versus bright gold, gunmetal versus bright white silver for a better simulation of expensive finishes.

Proportion, Proportion, Proportion

The scale of your bag in relation to the scale of your silhouette is everything. There should be a symmetry and balance between the two. Here's an example of proportion gone awry. A few years ago at Louis Vuitton in Paris, I watched a very petite woman buy a very oversized, bright red, patent leather Vernis Reade tote. Obviously elated, she left the store carrying it over her shoulder. I walked behind her down the Champs Elysées. The effect? She looked as though she was carrying an embossed stop sign that dwarfed her delicate frame.

Now, I'll tell on myself. A client sent me a Vuitton Pouchette. I had never owned anything quite this small and actually felt liberated by a bag meant for nothing more than a lipstick and a credit card. I carried it to a cocktail party where a man remarked: "My, you are a very large woman with a very small purse." Ouch. After I bopped him on the head with my tiny bag and told him to get me a drink, I realized I'd broken one of my own rules. At 6′ with broad shoulders (and a career as a stylist) I should have known better. I would have been better off with my trusty clutch—a midsize envelope that tucks under my arm.

putting shoes and bags together

It was easy before the 1960s: women simply bought shoes and hand-bags that matched. While an eclectic mix of colors and price levels can look very appealing and individualistic, it doesn't come off unless you pay attention to the references and details.

▶ **Are the tones compatible?** Warm with warm, cool with cool.
▶ **Are the shapes compatible and in proportion?** Rounded, feminine bags with feminine shoes, linear bag shapes with clean-lined, uncomplicated shoe styles, a small bag with a fine-lined or

delicate shoe, a midsized to large bag with a shoe that has a strong, simple look and a presence.

▶ **Are the details and the sensibility compatible?** For example, combining a shoe with tough looking metal buckles with a retro, girly bag, even if the colors work together, will sink your look. Mixing a crocodile bag with a lizard shoe is too much skin all around, mixing designer logos is flat-out bad taste.

sunglasses

Understandably, sunglasses can be a big part of the wardrobe I'll select for shoots, with celebrities in particular. If the subject is tough to shoot, the photographer can always fall back on the star in sunglasses shot for an image with a hint of mystery. If a young model simply doesn't know what to do with herself in front of the camera, I'll throw a pair of sunglasses on her to help with her shyness. They do something for us as both a glamorous new image and a shield. Wear your sunglasses in a shape that frames your face perfectly. I see girls every day all over Manhattan sporting styles ripped from the pages of some magazine's *hot sheet* that look as silly as party masks because the size and shapes are all wrong for their faces. As with everything you wear on your body, choosing the right shape is critical for the most flattering fit.

According to Rene Soltis, optometrist and spokesperson for the Vision Council of America, "although most faces are a combination of shapes and angles, each of us falls into one of seven basic shapes." Here's what she calls Facial Geometry 101. Carry this along to any sunglass counter or street stall.

▶ **Round:** Since the width and length of your face are approximately the same, try rectangular shapes to make your face appear longer and thinner.

▶ **Oval:** Your face has balanced proportions with height at your cheekbones and a chin that is slightly narrower than your forehead. Try varying sized oval shapes that are as wide or wider than the broadest part of your face.

▶ **Square:** You have a strong jawline, a broad forehead, and a wide chin and cheekbones with a width and length in proportion to one another. To make your face look longer, choose frames wider than the widest part of your face in horizontal or oval shapes, and look for styles that have weight on the top and that curve at the bottom to draw attention away from your jawline.

▶ **Oblong:** Your face is longer than it is wide, with straight features, maybe a long straight nose. Try frames with strong horizontal lines, round, deep, or low triangle shapes to make your face appear shorter and wider.

▶ **Heart:** You have a wide forehead and high cheekbones. Your face narrows gradually to the chin. Look for frames that are wider at the bottom and styles with rounded top and square bottom. Aviators may be a good choice. Light lenses and rimless styles soften width at the eye line.

▶ **Diamond:** Your face is narrow at your eyeline and jawline, with a small forehead and chin. You may have very high cheekbones. Look for straight square shapes, frames with a straight top and a curved bottom; or cat-eye and rimless frames to widen the appearance of your eyeline and forehead.

▶ **Triangle:** Your forehead is narrower and your face widens at your cheeks and chin. Look for square shapes with a strong line and emphasis on the top of the frame. Aviator styles with a straight top are a good choice to add width to your forehead and soften the lines of your cheeks and chin.

jewelry and watches

Nothing is more personal. No matter what they may have cost, the keepsakes that have a direct connection to our hearts are generally worn around our necks, our wrists, or on our fingers. Every girl will undoubtedly have some piece of jewelry that is immune to your stylist's guiding principles for jewelry and watches. That said, when you pick out jewelry or a watch for yourself, consider the following.

Scale, Scale, Scale

The scale of any ornamentation should be in balance and harmony with your body size and proportions. Here's what I'm talking about: I recently sat across the lunch table from a friend who is very tall and voluptuous. This girl has a great presence and yet her fine chain choker necklace—as thin as a strand of hair with a charm the size of a Tic-Tac—did not. The necklace, while pretty, looked nearly invisible on her statuesque frame. Let your scale guide the scale of any jewelry you choose.

▶ **Tall and voluptuous girls** who prefer dainty jewelry should consider wearing groups of necklaces that work together for a cascade effect to create more surface with the fine texture. Try thin but large hoops for more impact. Take full advantage of your stature by wearing strong, oversized pieces where they flatter your focal points, like an important cuff bracelet or a stack of thin bangles to create surface interest; cascades of large, bold beads, or a few long strands; cocktail rings sized for maximum impact or long, full drop earrings. Choose a watch from the men's department or a women's style that is similarly scaled. A tiny watch will look insignificant on you. The most attractive thing about large-scale jewelry is that one piece with impact is all you may need to finish an outfit.

▶ **Petite girls** are always advised to wear minimal, clean and undersized jewelry. Not overwhelming a petite frame with too many accessories is the right idea but I've often broken the rules for petite women by choosing oversized earrings, for example, but designed of ultrafine wire or chain; large hoops in very thin wire or a lacey, midsized pendant-shaped earring; an armful of ultrathin bangles, or two or three strands of necklaces varying in size from small to medium. The amount of surface created by the materials counts as much as the size of the piece. Look at the size of your wrist and hand and choose a watch that has a flattering proportion. A key consideration for petites of all sizes: Accessorize a focal point and leave it at that. Keep it simple.

▶ **Full bustlines** benefit from necklaces that fall at the base of the throat to midchest so that the focal point falls above your breasts. Raise your pendant necklaces so that they fall within this range.

▶ **Full necks** are often advised to wear button earrings and stay away from long earrings as they create a focal point at your neck. I've yet to meet a stylish woman under sixty-five who yearns for a pair of button earrings. I've found that girls with full necks can look very saucy in long earrings that create a vertical line raising the eye up and down. Avoid round or full shapes that create a horizontal line at your neck. Replace those buttons with simple diamond studs, for example.

Go for Authenticity

For costume jewelry and belts look for authenticity. Go for anything real at any price you can afford rather than the faux offerings on those spinning carousels in the department stores. Anything that looks stamped out and mass manufactured can tarnish your look overall (the subliminal message: you have no imagination). Sure, a gold or silver hoop, a pearl stud, or versatile link necklace or bracelet are natural finds at department stores or at specialty shops, like Agatha, which update status classics, but when you want an ethnic or retro reference at a price go to the source. Stores that import goods from India, Mexico, Turkey, Morocco, Tibet, China, as well as flea markets and secondhand stores are the sources for unique things. Check leather stores that offer a choice of custom buckles for their belts. Always comb small independent stores for jewelry designs by undiscovered talent; string your own beads. Wherever you can, *customize, personalize, put your own stamp on things.*

Context

Another universal truth about innately stylish girls is that they understand that accessories have a context; certain pieces of clothing and certain pieces of jewelry are meant to exist together, others are not. Like the television actress I met at a cocktail party wearing a simple black sheath and stilettos with an outsized American Indian squash blossom necklace covering her dress front. A case of mixed metaphors as the rustic effect of the necklace clashed with the urban sophistication of her dress. Or the girl I clocked on the subway one morning wearing a cotton khaki pantsuit, gym sneakers, and a pair of long and lacey shoulder dusting earrings (not so coincidentally this misstep occurred on the heels of an *InStyle* spread on just such earrings). Or my art director friend who spent a small fortune on a long fringed belt off the runway that she read was a *must have* then asked me what to wear it with. We went through her closet of very classic things and determined that she would have to buy an entire outfit for the belt. This kind of ass-backwards accessorizing happens all the time.

When you read in the magazines that an elbow-length leather glove is *hot*, that outsized chandelier earrings like the dazzlers worn at the Oscars are *hot*, that mink stoles for day are *hot*, and that buying any of these things can update last year's clothing, go have a good long look in your closet before you buy into the hype and spend your money. Understand the **context in which those accessory ideas have been presented.** Log on to Style.com and take in the entire sensibility of the collections that have featured these things in the first place. If you already own a few similar silhouettes and styles as the looks these same accessories are meant to finish, and the scale of the accessory is right for you, then buying a few trendy accessories each season is the ideal way to keep your wardrobe looking current.

One of the most promising trends in jewelry is that women no longer wait around to receive serious jewelry as gifts. Shopping statistics indicate that *self-purchase* or sales that represent women purchasing their own diamonds, colored stones, and antique pieces increase annually. According to Sally Morrison, director of the Diamond Information Center "the most popular self-purchases are right-hand fashion rings and earrings, followed by necklaces." If you've decided that now is the time to invest in an important piece of jewelry, whether everyday diamond studs, a colored-stone cocktail ring, or an estate piece then familiarize yourself with these guidelines.

Diamond Purchases

The value of a diamond is determined by four factors: cut, color, clarity, and carat weight. Sally Morrison walks us through the details.

4 C's of Buying a Diamond

▶ **Cut:** The way a diamond is cut and how many facets it has (the tiny planes that create angles on its surface). The cut influences a diamond's fire: its brilliance and sparkle.

▶ **Color:** To the naked eye, most diamonds appear white but virtually all stones have a trace of color. Diamonds are graded by measuring the degree to which a stone approaches colorlessness. A jeweler will describe the color of a diamond on a letter scale beginning with D (colorless) and moving through the alphabet. D, E, and F stones are the most expensive because they are the most rare. Bottom line: a well-cut stone with good clarity in all color grades can look great in an earring or right-hand ring for example.

▶ **Clarity:** Almost all diamonds contain naturally occurring small blemishes, called *inclusions,* which can be seen under powerful magnification or a ten-power jeweler's loupe. Diamonds with the fewest inclusions are graded as VVS1 or VVS2. Diamonds on the other end of the scale are graded as I1 or I3. The fewer inclusions, the more valuable the stone.

▶ **Carat:** The standard system of measuring weight of all precious stones. One carat (.2 grams) is divided into 100 points. A diamond of 25 points is described as a quarter of a carat, or .25 carats, and a diamond of 50 points is described as a half carat or .50 carats, and so on.

Sally advises that there is a fifth C—confidence in the jeweler. "Ask any friends whose jewelry you admire what jeweler they've shopped with. Any jeweler who sells you a diamond should be very knowledgeable about diamonds. You can also contact either the Jewelers of America (800-223-0673) or the American Gem Society (800-341-6214) for jeweler recommendations in your area."

Colored Stone Purchases

Brazil is renowned for producing some of the world's most beautiful colored stones. To gather information for colored stone purchases I asked Andrea Hansen, marketing director of Brazil's H. Stern Jewelers for advice. According to Andrea "popular colored stones like aquamarine, pink and green tourmalines, topaz, and amethyst, for example, are graded against a standard of master cuts for their shade and overall quality."

▶ **Color:** "The deeper and more brilliant the color of a stone, the greater its value. Even though very light stones move in and out of fashion, for an enduring investment your best bet is to choose a vivid, color-saturated look in a stone you love."

▶ **Inclusions:** "Be careful that you cannot see any visible internal cracks (inclusions) or small black marks where dirt has been trapped within a crack. For overall investment, choose a stone with the least inclusions."

Purchasing Antique, Vintage, and Estate Jewelry

If ever there was a shopping pursuit for the woman who loves a treasure hunt, collecting antique and vintage jewelry is it. There simply is no better way to individualize your look than with a unique accessory you won't see on anyone else.

I've been hooked since college when a weekly flea market near campus caught my attention. I'd comb the jewelry stalls most Sundays, as they proved to be a trove of unusual costume jewelry from the thirties, forties, and fifties. As I trained my eye, I felt more confident about looking things over carefully and asking questions. My budget each week? $20, but it was big money to me then and I considered my purchases as carefully as if I'd been spending $2,000. It's a passion I've indulged ever since. Do I have some kind of world-class collection? No, I do not. I buy what I love providing the condition is very good, the scale is right for me, and, most important, that I feel an inexplicable tug when I put it on. *If it just feels right* than it has value to me and that's all I worry about. That said, I've enlisted the advice of a respected dealer to share some tips with you.

Melody Rodgers' New York City shop Terry Rodgers and Melody is a jewel box filled with a beautifully edited collection of antique and vintage estate pieces. When I want truly unique accessories for a fashion shoot I visit Melody. I asked how the average girl with a taste for the unique and original look of antique jewelry can best begin her search: "Experts will always tell you that you must first consider the value of a piece based on authenticity, condition, and investment. While these are important considerations, you should also experience what I call the gasp factor. Do you have an immediate visual reaction to a piece? Shopping for old things is not a pursuit for the Internet shopper. Choosing *antiques* (pieces 100 years or older), *vintage* (at least 50 but under 100), and *estate pieces* (meaning anything old or new that is preowned and has been purchased by the dealer from an estate) is a completely visual and visceral experience. You have to touch things, feel the weight in your hand, and try them on. You'll either feel a connection to a piece or you won't.

"First, clean out your jewelry box," Melody advises. (Yes, more cleaning and organization.) "Edit out anything you've grown out of and consider the things that have an enduring quality for you. The scale and metal colors of these pieces can be a good guiding principle as you begin to look."

▶ **Establish your price range:** "Even if you have $50 to spend ask the dealer to show you things in your range. No matter what you spend, look for wearability and have a real passion for the look of the piece. These are the factors that endure," says Rodgers.

▶ **Ask a lot of questions:** "Talk to a dealer about the age/period of a piece. What can they tell you about the craftsmanship and materials used? Look things over carefully taking into consideration the condition of the stones and of the metal fittings holding them in place. Examine the back of the piece—can you see any subtle differences in color that would indicate that it may have had a little 'reconstructive surgery?' If you suspect so, ask the dealer if the piece has had repairs."

▶ **Develop your own style:** "Don't worry about what's hot or collectible at the moment, since old periods move in and out of fashion in the same way that clothing trends do. Pay attention to the overall look of a piece. All of the design components should come together to create something balanced. Look for period distinction. There is no point in shopping vintage for something as contemporary as a tennis bracelet, for example."

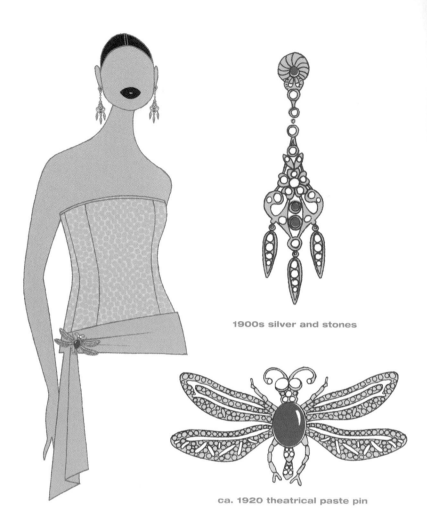

1900s silver and stones

ca. 1920 theatrical paste pin

▶ **Change the color:** "If you find something in sterling silver and wish it were gold or that a shade of gold was more flattering for your skin tone, have it dipped," Melody explains. "This is not expensive and there are dozens of shades of gold to choose from. You do have to keep up with wear, however, and have things redipped periodically."

▶ **Shopping for companion pieces:** "When you want to find a piece with both a scale and design that is compatible to something you already own, perhaps a pair of earrings to complement a necklace, for example, always have the piece with you in your search. Show it to the dealer so that they can help you with the right look in periods and materials."

▶ **Never rule out costume jewelry:** According to Melody, "Early costume pieces demonstrate incredible craftsmanship. Many pieces produced between the wars in the 1930s and '40s are not only handmade and produced from good quality metals and imitation stones but are actually quite valuable." Things of this quality simply can't be duplicated today at the price.

▶ **Avoid reproduction antiques:** When you see more than one of the same piece or if the metals and stones look new, they probably are. "Reproductions have less value so it's better to keep looking and, again, ask the dealer if something is a reproduction," advises Melody.

▶ **Trust your instincts:** Like any sales relationship, if you like the way a dealer edits their collection and like the quality of what they buy, frequent their shop, stall, or table and get to know them. "Always beware the hard sell," says Rodgers. "If a dealer pressures you about a sale either walk away and think about it or ask if they will accept a refundable deposit. Never make a hurried or pressured decision you may regret later."

scarves

Scarves are often overlooked. Have a few good-quality square scarves in your arsenal. Look for prints that incorporate skin-flattering cosmetic colors (red, orange, pink, coral) in the pattern. Any morning you look as though you need a blood transfusion, throw on a crew neck top and wrap a scarf around your neck, choker-style.

My personal favorite scarf-tying trick: Fold a large square in half (form a triangle). Fold the pointed edge into the center, cover that with the smooth edge, and fold again until you arrive at a width that is flattering for your neck. Tie the scarf in a knot at the base of your neck and let the ends hang down your back. The effect is a smooth, uncomplicated pop of color for your face. Dab on a little blush and lipstick that pull out a cosmetic tone in the design. *Voilà.*

Add a few more large squares or oblongs to your stash and you'll always have an emergency belt or sash, and a head wrap or bandanna for wretched hair days. Nothing is more affordable and useful to a girl on a budget than a cache of scarves. You can always find them in bins at vintage stores for reasonable prices.

I am always on the hunt for squares and oblongs that will flatter my skin tone or that include browns, blacks, and strong pops of "trend" brights for belt substitutes.

Own a wrap as well. This is where the ubiquitous pashmina can come in handy. Inspect the quality carefully, however. Invest in cashmere or cashmere and wool blends. Many bargain cashmere and silk blends pill after a few wearings. Choose a color that makes your skin tone sing and wear it as a neutral. Very useful wrapped several times around your neck for warmth, an instant solution for cold shoulders in a dress, and a dandy blanket on airplanes.

hats

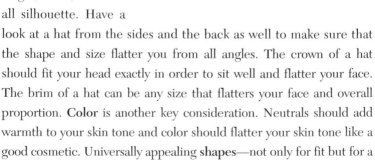

Any hat, from a cotton bucket you wear in the rain to a felt fedora, can make or break your look, since it can either increase or decrease the appearance/size of your head in relation to the rest of your body. When you try one on, look at yourself in a full-length mirror (three-way, ideally) to be sure it looks in **proportion** to your height, frame, and overall silhouette. Have a look at a hat from the sides and the back as well to make sure that the shape and size flatter you from all angles. The crown of a hat should fit your head exactly in order to sit well and flatter your face. The brim of a hat can be any size that flatters your face and overall proportion. **Color** is another key consideration. Neutrals should add warmth to your skin tone and color should flatter your skin tone like a good cosmetic. Universally appealing **shapes**—not only for fit but for a noncostumed look on the street—the beret, the bucket with either a short or medium brim, the small-brimmed fedora, wide brims, floppy brims, and the classic golf or newsboy cap.

> **TIP:** One absolute *no* in hat proportion: a brim wider than your shoulders!

belts

Aside from creating a focal point at the waist or hips, belts can be used to elongate the look of your torso and smooth over a full abdomen. A medium to wide belt dropped to just below your navel creates an optical illusion, a sort of camouflage effect over the fullness and pulls the eye downward giving the torso above a longer line. A monochromatic or tonal match of belt and bottom is a tried and true trick for a slimming definition. The most universally flattering belts or sash belts of any width will have a supple, moldable quality and are *contoured*, meaning that the back of the belt is slightly wider than the front and sits higher on your backside while the front sits lower. Any sash that can be wrapped and adjusted to your individual shape for a sensuous, curvy fit is a good belt to add to your wardrobe.

> **TIP:** This trick works for most every woman and can visually shave off five pounds. Choose a smooth T-shirt or lightweight sweater and wear it over a dark or darker tonal bottom with a smooth waistband. Choosing a soft belt or contoured belt in either the same color or a close tonal match as your top, position it just at or below your navel so that it is flush over your abdomen. A belt of 2½ to 4 inches is ideal here. Make sure that your belt covers the hem of your top. The effect—one long line—is also an ideal underpinning when worn under a topper that clears your bottom.

Oh, and one last thought before you grab your credit cards. To paraphrase the late, incomparable fashion doyenne Diana Vreeland: always take off one accessory before you head out the door. More is seldom more.

afterword

A few years ago, your stylist's services were auctioned at a charity benefit. The package: a consultation consisting of a closet sweep and serious shopping time. Weeks later, Mrs. X, my client, led me into a capacious walk-in closet heaving with clothes. And not just any clothes, I might add. Over the last five years, whatever the magazines had promoted as must-have luxuries, Mrs. X had them. Like flash cards, she could tell me which actress had worn the same look to an opening, which young socialites favored this designer, and which dress both Sarah Jessica Parker's character on *Sex and the City* and Jennifer Aniston from *Friends* had worn for a pushed-up, Italian movie star silhouette. I should interject here that Mrs. X's body did not resemble the silhouette or proportions of either actress.

It is an understatement to say that Mrs. X had a touch of fashion schizophrenia. Her wardrobe was all over the map. As she tried on one verbatim head-to-toe designer look after another, no sense of the woman wearing the clothes emerged. The clothes were wearing the woman. Lost in luxury, Mrs. X had looks galore but few simple indispensables with which to pair them or to tone things down a bit. No old favorites to throw into the mix for an individual stamp. Hers was a hypercoordinated attempt at style but, in look after expensive look, none of it really flattered her. Mrs. X didn't believe in herself in her clothes and neither did I. After a few glasses of wine, she confessed that salespeople could talk her into anything because she was intimidated by not really knowing about fashion. She said she "loved knowing that someone famous had worn something because it meant that it was right." Right on whom? Not Mrs. X, it turned out.

Now, I'll allow that Mrs. X is an example of fashion victim in the extreme, but let's use her closet and her choices as a case study of sorts: What was missing? *For starters, a clear sense of her body.* Although choked with enough luxury swag to fill a small store, her closet contained very few pieces that worked for her frame (type A, by the way). For Mrs. X, for you, and for me, as for every woman, the rock-solid foundation of personal style is an understanding of your silhouette and proportions. This is where it all begins. Yes, I'm flogging this point yet again, because it is the simple and not so secret element of creating a signature style. Keep what works for your body in mind and in your closet and you are well on your way.

Every girl needs a few *uniforms*. No, this is not the point in our conversation when I'll tell you that you should find two or three pieces that work and buy them in every color. Rather, concentrate on the focal points you've identified and on the silhouettes from your edited shopping list. These are the pieces that are going to make you feel great whenever you wear them. Any day. Always. Then brazenly, shamelessly work current versions of these same uniforms into your repertoire from now on. Fill in the colors, the textures, and the trends that flatter you and keep your look evolving each season and over time. After all, this same philosophy has worked for the most admired and widely acknowledged style icons of our time.

To flip through archival photos of some of the female fashion icons we revere—Jackie, Audrey, Marilyn—is to look at women who understood the power of their uniforms. The most obvious place to start is with Jacqueline Kennedy Onassis who, from her White House years to her life as a New York book editor, favored the same, essentially A-line, silhouettes. Hers was an uncomplicated, linear, and graphic style, often in combinations of black and white. Her small upper body was defined by simple necklines; the cut of her skimming, trim jackets and her signature turtlenecks created the illusion of broader shoulders and accentuated her long neck. Her hemlines reflected the season but avoided the extremes—she knew what lengths best flattered her legs. Her trademark oversized sunglasses punctuated her streamlined look.

Or look at Marilyn Monroe, America's modern Aphrodite and a woman who dressed to accentuate every inch of what was, at times, a size 14 in the pattern making of her day: low V-necklines, a fitted or cinched waist, and curvy bottoms defined her silhouette; on the set in that gingham shirt tied up at her waist and her custom fit dungarees molding to her hips and thighs; in pencil skirts and cropped jackets over sweaters; or in that famous (and endlessly imitated) white halter dress blowing above the subway grate. Figure-hugging silhouettes defined her bombshell style. It worked for her shape and she rarely changed that combination of proportions or her uniforms throughout her life.

Naturally, Audrey Hepburn defines a timeless standard for women of all ages. Her sylph's frame was any fashion designer's dream. Collaborating with her on and off screen, Hubert de Givenchy created clothes that invariably fit tightly across her bodice. Necklines and shoulders were cut to accentuate, even exaggerate, her shoulders and swan neck. Her waistlines were cinched and defined in the fifties and her shift dresses skimmed her body in the sixties but we never lost sight of that tiny waist or those dancer's legs. From the gamine style of leggings and ballet flats to *haute couture* gowns, the same combination of focal points prevailed in her wardrobe throughout her life.

A modern example of a successful uniform is Oprah Winfrey's on-camera wardrobe. Her savvy combinations of current and body-conscious shapes in monochromatic or tonal combinations, interesting necklines that create a focal point at her shoulders and neck, and well-proportioned killer accessories, define her look, her uniform.

Here's another example of a woman with a winning uniform. Polly Allen Mellen, a respected fashion editor for *Vogue* and *Allure* and a protégée of Diana Vreeland is someone whose style I've admired as an example of one's image and uniform successfully evolving over time. In 1989, I spotted Polly, (in her sixties) walking into a fashion show. She was wearing the *au courant* black leather Perfecto motorcycle jacket of the moment. A shape and proportion (cropped) that flattered her frame perfectly. How did she pull this off? With a pair of flawlessly cut, slim, black wool trousers, a white T-shirt, and unadorned black slippers. She was both timeless and completely of the moment. And unmistakably comfortable in her own skin. I'll mention that her signature steel gray bob cut punctuated the right-now simplicity of her look.

Now, let's flash forward ten years to a 1999 Armani fashion show. Polly, front row and looking simply great in a Gaultier denim jacket lined with fur. Essentially the same cut as that Perfecto of ten years earlier, worn with a current version of her knife-cut pants, white T-shirt, a new take on the slippers, and her bob in place. I thought to myself at the time: same as ten years ago but completely of the minute. Wear whatever you want at any age, just wear it with conviction. Conviction comes easily when you know what flatters your body type. Anchor those trends with pieces that are ultimately flattering, ageless. and timeless.

IS IT TRUE THAT GREAT PERSONAL STYLE—*chic*, if you will—is innate? Yes, absolutely, but it can also be learned and refined. For some women, putting themselves together well is purely instinctual. Their eyes are naturally drawn to the right shapes, colors, the right proportions and scale. Shopping and dressing well are like breathing for them. If this is not you, so what? Remember this: every style icon has had a mentor or two. For Jackie, it was the *Vogue* editor Diana Vreeland; for Marilyn, Hollywood costume designers like Edith Head; for Audrey, Givenchy recognized and further refined her natural style and grace. Smart women have always transformed an interest in clothes into a signature style by asking questions and seeking out good advice; by watching what's happening in the world and on the streets, as well as on the runways and in magazines.

Your everyday personal style begins and ends with a sense of yourself. At the risk of sounding like a pop psychologist, in the dressing room there is no mistaking a woman who likes herself—at any size—and who understands what flatters her best. She dresses her body as a reflection of that self-regard. There is no faking this part of your psychology. Every stitch you wear is an unspoken statement of your self-image. Watch the woman on the street who takes a sensual pleasure in her clothes. The fit, the skim, and drape do all the talking. Louder still, the silent scream of the woman who throws on clothes grudgingly, without pleasure *and to avoid arrest.*

Here are a few more things that all of us need to know:

Women with style possess a kind of filter to help them sift through new trends and ideas. They buy things very discriminatingly, a few key pieces at a time, to add the seasonal luster that sparks all the existing favorites in their wardrobes. It doesn't matter whether they're shopping at Neiman Marcus or at Old Navy, they're not seduced by something (even at a disposable price) unless it really works for them in all the ways we've discussed throughout the book. Develop your filter and watch how quickly your wardrobe looks more focused;

how well the new things you add to the mix—a few pieces at a time—work with what you already own. Think about it. You wouldn't decorate your house or apartment in a few days with a phone call to one catalogue or a stop at one store and expect to create a look that reflected your personality, your individuality. The best wardrobes develop over time, pieces at a time, and they last.

Few things are more self-affirming than dressing well. Women with style don't fall back on the current climate of "no more fashion edicts" as an excuse to live in terry cloth sweatpants and hoodies. They take pleasure in wearing real clothes because they take pleasure in their bodies in clothes. They put a bit of thought into whatever they wear wherever they wear it. It doesn't matter whether it's a pair of old jeans and a white shirt from the Gap combined with a few good accessories or the deceptive wrapper of a good-looking coat worn just to run errands (and to cover those terry sweatpants) or a dab of concealer here and a little lipstick there to brighten up the face. Or a pretty scarf or a cheeky hat to cover their filthy hair (yes, even to walk the dog). Give thought to everything you wear, not just the pieces you invest in for work or to go out in the evening.

Stylish women understand how to mix it up. They appreciate contradiction as a way to define a look. This is the woman who never buys the coordinated look, wrapped and ready to go. She draws on her interests and shops at every price, maybe choosing a hyperfeminine shape in a menswear tweed or wearing something classic (and ten years old) with the trendiest piece she owns. She understands that the success of the mix relies not only on fit and proportions but also on how the references relate to one another. She can mix patterns, make old and new work together, combine feminine with masculine.

Stylish women know that taste is not a dirty word. The "T" word has been somewhat maligned over the last decade or so. To describe someone as *tasteful* has come to mean a style that is too safe or, if not a snore, perhaps too done, too matched and coordinated. All together, a little too *jolie madame* to be considered stylish. Nonsense.

Good taste is also eclectic; individual; eccentric. Having taste is knowing the difference between subtle sexuality and vulgarity. That more is not more. That the suggestion of the body in clothes and a well-placed focal point to reveal some skin is far more powerful than anything crotch high or navel grazing. To tack a celebrity face onto this perception, think of Nicole Kidman in jeans and a Marc Jacobs jacket or on the red carpet in St. Laurent and wearing only the jewelry essential to the look. The girl has great taste. Then think of the Hilton sisters and their train-wreck style. I rest my case.

Stylish women know how to adapt a current look to suit their age. Unless they are in their teens or their twenties, they never dress like girls in their teens and twenties. And they know to never abandon their eye for a season's current accessories as a way of infusing their wardrobes with the right quotient of right now. They also understand that the cut and line of their clothing flatters their bodies—at any age or size—and requires minimal complication. They have distilled the alchemy of personal style to its essence. And they walk out the door every day with the self-assurance that they look damn good in their clothes.

As Yves St. Laurent said, fashion fades, style is eternal. ●

acknowledgments

My thanks to the following individuals for their contributions, support, and enthusiasm:

My agent Tanya McKinnon, Mary Evans Inc; my editor, Lauren Marino; Anja Kroencke for beautiful illustrations; designer Susi Oberhelman for her marvelous eye; John at Judy Casey; Mitchell Gross; Alexandra Boos; Monica Willis; Lars Nord; Kevin Mancuso; Bobbi Brown; Sonia Kashuk; Dida Paraschivoiu; Melody Rodgers, Terry Rodgers & Melody; Rebecca Apsan, La Petite Coquette; Valerie McKaskill, VICA; Andrea Hansen, H.Stern Jewelers; Carson Glover, A Diamond Is Forever; Troi Ollivierre, for his magic wand; and Belle.